T0209986

UNFOLD YOUR SOUL

A MEMOIR

THEA WOODS

BALBOA.PRESS

A DIVISION OF HAY HOUSE

Copyright © 2020 Thea Woods.

All rights reserved. No part of this book may be used or reproduced by
any means, graphic, electronic, or mechanical, including photocopying,
recording, taping or by any information storage retrieval system
without the written permission of the author except in the case
of brief quotations embodied in critical articles and reviews.

Balboa Press books may be ordered through booksellers or by contacting:

Balboa Press
A Division of Hay House
1663 Liberty Drive
Bloomington, IN 47403
www.balboapress.com
1 (877) 407-4847

Because of the dynamic nature of the Internet, any web addresses or
links contained in this book may have changed since publication and
may no longer be valid. The views expressed in this work are solely those
of the author and do not necessarily reflect the views of the publisher,
and the publisher hereby disclaims any responsibility for them.

The author of this book does not dispense medical advice or prescribe the use
of any technique as a form of treatment for physical, emotional, or medical
problems without the advice of a physician, either directly or indirectly. The
intent of the author is only to offer information of a general nature to help
you in your quest for emotional and spiritual well-being. In the event you use
any of the information in this book for yourself, which is your constitutional
right, the author and the publisher assume no responsibility for your actions.

Any people depicted in stock imagery provided by Getty Images are
models, and such images are being used for illustrative purposes only.
Certain stock imagery © Getty Images.

Print information available on the last page.

ISBN: 978-1-9822-4259-6 (sc)
ISBN: 978-1-9822-4260-2 (e)

Balboa Press rev. date: 02/26/2020

To Oliver, Terence, and Jacob.
Thank you for reminding me, each in your own way,
that the only delights meant to be imprisoned
in a box are chocolates.

CONTENTS

PART II – Lit from Within

PART III – The Magnificent Maple

FOREWORD

When I was only fifteen years old, I was, for various reasons, already in a lot of psychic pain and hungry for a path out of my suffering. One afternoon, I was walking across the streets of my New York City neighborhood in a pre-Christmas snowfall, the warmth and conviviality of the season only serving to heighten my sense of isolation and failure. Suddenly, a man thrust something into my hands. I unrolled it, expecting a flier for a new Chinese restaurant—but instead it was a copy of a poem.

For that one afternoon, my local drugstore was passing out copies of a poem called "Disiderata" by Max Ehrmann that begins, "Go placidly amid the noise and haste, and remember what peace there may be in silence," and ends many stanzas later with, "And whether or not it is clear to you, no doubt the universe is unfolding as it should. Therefore, be at peace with God, whatever you conceive Him to be. And whatever your labors and aspirations, in the noisy confusion of life, keep peace in your soul. With all its sham, drudgery and broken dreams, it is still a beautiful world. Be cheerful. Strive to be happy."

Standing in the heart of the Upper East Side, a place renowned for its prioritization of surface appearance over authentic expression, I felt like I had found a message in a bottle meant just for me. I taped those miraculous words up over my bed and read them to myself every morning upon waking and every night before bed. They became my beacon that told me that I was not alone, something greater than me was guiding me, and if I just trusted and leaned into it, I would be carried.

I had a similar feeling upon first reading the book you hold in your hands. Through Thea's brave and vulnerable account of her own moments of connection with the divine and All That Is, I felt myself refreshed in my confidence that there is an enormous sea of love out there waiting for us—our only job is to tap into it.

Chapter by chapter, Thea lays out the harrowing journey of her childhood—and the spiritual awakening and transformation that allowed her to transcend her conditioning and find the expansive love that is the birthright of all of us.

I am so excited for you to read this book and go on this journey with Thea. I am hoping you come away from it as I did—renewed, reinvigorated, and filled with a desire to find that connection for yourself to that space of divine love.

Nicola Kraus
Author of *The Nanny Diaries*
September 2019

PREFACE

I would like to thank my family for providing me with a home and a life full of adventure and opportunities. My mom recalls the day I arrived on their doorstep; no stuffed animal, no blankey, just the clothes on my back. My family provided me with all the things I'd never had. I challenged my new parents for many months (possibly even years) with my distrusting behaviour, and my parents (specifically my mom) rose to the occasion with steadfast love and determination. She showed up every time, no matter how challenging the situation. I am forever grateful to both my parents and my sister for their love and willingness to take me in and take me on—no easy feat. I have seen many remarkable parts of the world on our travels and have been spoiled with the love of family in more ways than one.

This book is a memoir, and it reflects my recollection of experiences in my life and how they shaped me into the person I am today. I have done my best to tell a truthful story. I recognise that other people's memories of the events in this book may be slightly different than mine. Time erodes the precision of events and memory repairs or distorts them. It has never been my intention to hurt anyone in the writing of this book; I only seek the truth, my truth. I regret any unintentional harm resulting from the publishing of *Unfold Your Soul*. All names have been changed or omitted to respect individuals and their privacy.

ACKNOWLEDGMENT

I would like to thank my editor Nicola Kraus, who, after reading my first draft, kind-heartedly informed me that all first drafts were crummy and mine was no different. Nicola encouraged me to keep my butt in the chair, though, and to see the process through to the end. I am grateful for her wealth of experience, her uplifting words of optimism, and her sense of humour. Thank you, Nicola–you are far more than my editor! My gratitude to you is immeasurable.

Thanks to my friends Lanije, Martina, and Mamma C for listening and holding a safe space for me to be vulnerable. Your unconditional support and encouragement comforted me throughout the writing process and ignited my eagerness to carry on.

Thank you to my greatest teacher in contrast, my father, and my greatest awakener, my son. It is because of your steadfast presence in my life that I was able to begin the ever-expanding process of unfolding my soul. I am eternally grateful to you both.

Dearly Beloved, we have gathered here today
To get through this thing called life
Electric word life
It means forever and that's a mighty long time
But I'm here to tell you, there's something else.

—Prince, "Let's Go Crazy"

PART I

THE DEEP SLEEP

CHAPTER ONE

1969-1989

"You've always had the power, my dear, you just had to learn it for yourself."

—Glinda, the Good Witch,
The Wizard of Oz

Whether I will be the heroine of my own life is yet to be known. All I can say is that I've shown up with determined participation in my own unique way. If you enjoy stories that are faithful to the illusion of the common dream, then you may wish to move on.

People talk about young Souls and old Souls, but from my place of understanding, it's more the awareness a Soul chooses to experience in their lifetime that dictates their experiences. My definition of the Soul is simply this; it is the vast ocean of consciousness apart from our mortal frame that belongs specifically to you in every dimensional experience you choose to have. The Soul cannot be owned, yet it is fluid and inherited. Like Nature, the Soul is transcendental, ever growing and unfolding. I have no doubt that the complexity of the Soul is immense and quite possibly limitless. Certainly, in this lifetime, my awareness of all things related to the Soul has been shaken, not stirred—a lifetime filled with a compelling cast of characters and curious and thought-provoking narratives.

Growing up, I kept very quiet about the things I witnessed

and experienced. If I was out of my mind it was OK with me, I just didn't want anyone else to know. I will share a few of the most outlandish happenings with you in this book because I think by opening up about my own unique *awairdness* (awareness of weird things) it may give other people permission to do the same, to share their singular perspectives and encounters. It is these experiences, great or small, curious or fantastic, which help unfurl and broaden our consciousness, the intelligence beyond our biological and mental faculties. When I speak of the Soul, higher consciousness, or Soul-self, I am referring to them as one and the same. A Soul that has never incarnated on Earth, or anywhere else for that matter, may not choose to have full access to its awareness, but I don't want to rule it out. It seems from my place of understanding (which might be very limited, in the grand scheme of things) that the more experience a Soul has, the more of a repertoire of awareness it builds. And this seems to happen incrementally with each lifetime.

Untethered Buoy

My Earth-bound voyage began on July 20, 1969 in a cottage on Mississagua Lake in Ontario, Canada. The very night Armstrong bounced gravity-free on the gleaming rock in the sky we call the moon. That evening, my biological mother, Natalie, twenty-six years old, mixed more than just cocktails with a reckless, self-serving joe. A momentous day in world history and an enormously consequential one for Nat. One wee drink led to one great baby nine months later. Glorious me. These two events were quite separate and yet connected all the same.

Nat had a birth plan in place and was prepared to put me up for adoption the minute my presence was proclaimed.

However, like so many mothers before her, upon seeing me she relinquished her plan and asked to be given time to make suitable living arrangements to bring me home. For the first six months of my life, I lived in foster care. When I was approximately seven months old, I was handed back to Nat.

My biological father was aware of my arrival on this blue and white marble but did not celebrate with ceremonial cigars. Like the character *The Man with No Name*, he rode into town, shot the place up, and rode off, leaving a holy mess in his wake. He refused to participate in my upbringing and did not give Nat a single penny for my livelihood. Nat's immediate family were sickened at the idea of a *bastard* child and feared the shame it would bring to them. Nat's mom, Ruth, was all too familiar with family shame, as her own mother was the result of an affair Ruth's grandmother had with an indigenous man. In the late 1800s, this was blasphemous.

History repeating itself, Nat was shunned by both her mom and dad and received no support emotionally or financially. This was 1970 and there was a significant stigma back then around conceiving out of wedlock. This shame was then transferred to me at a very young age through various experiences of neglect, from being turned away at Ruth's house on Christmas day to my mom being too spirited during Happy Hour and forgetting to pick me up after work.

From the minute I was conceived, my song was a solitary one. After foster care, I was handed back to Mother, then to her friend's mom, back to Mother, then back to a foster care stranger, and then finally, after two and a half years of this vacillating rhumba, I was put up for adoption. I always felt an underlying sense of not being wanted and some confusion over where I belonged, if I was loved unconditionally, and whether I was accepted.

I'm not sure exactly what made my mother decide to give me up, but whatever the case, the legal records show that in

1972 she was in court stating her inability to provide me with what she deemed to be a "wholesome" life.

The dreaded day of my hand-over to Children's Aid arrived, and a torrential downpour heralded my departure. My mother was sick to her stomach with emotion and could not take me herself. She called her trusted friend, my godmother, Joyce, and asked her to chaperon me. The sky continued to spill gems of rain in an incessant, heavyhearted melody. When we finally arrived, Joyce gave me a squeeze and hastily said her goodbyes. I met Joyce many decades later and she recalled the events of that day with a quivering bottom lip. Joyce then headed to a hotel lobby bar to pick up the shattered remains of Nat who, following a deep depression, would go on to die from cancer twelve years later.

As for me, my retrograde rhumba continued. I was thrown back into foster care with a new set of strangers, and it wasn't until six months later that a permanent home for me was found.

Lifeline

In the spring of 1972, Children's Aid approved a family for me, one that I had met with a few times, and they seemed eager to adopt me. I was going to have a forever home. At last. A mom, a dad, and even an older sister. The following seven years were tremendously happy ones, albeit challenging at first, as I was cautious and suspicious that it would all end in a flash, as my brief history had taught me. My new mom understood the demands I was placing on her daily, but she embraced me with love and determination and stayed the course no matter what I threw her way. She provided me with the dependability and security I yearned for. I had my own bedroom, clothes, food at regular hours, bath-time, and bedtime stories. Finally, a normal childhood.

Slowly over time, I began to trust adults again and the world at large. My new best friend lived across the street, and she, too, was adopted. I was happy to know that there were other kids like me out there. With our neighbourhood friends, we roamed and played freely in the streets and nearby park, and those seven years were some of the happiest of my life. I have vivid memories of playing catch with my dad on the front lawn and eating hot dogs and cake on my sixth birthday with my friends. My dad's first love was sailing, so whenever there was a light summer breeze, we were swept off on his boat. Saturday mornings were bathed in the aroma of my mom's homemade granola and it soaked my being in the warmth and comfort of family.

The Coin of Life

In 1978, at the age of eight, I was a vibrant bundle of golden locks with a Pepsodent smile. My mom gave me and my older sister a couple of dimes and quarters on Saturdays so we could go buy candy or save up for a rainy day. I always spent my coins on sugary junk, while my sister diligently popped hers into her piggy bank. We were then, and are today, opposites in so many ways—contrasting personalities within the same family unit. On this particularly cheerful Saturday, I bounced like Tigger to the corner store in great anticipation of my sugar rush. I carefully selected my sweets of choice and then skipped out with my handful of happiness.

I chewed off a SweeTART from my candy necklace and noticed I still had a dime in my pocket. Its shiny surface sparkled and drew me in. On one side, there was a face—(the) Queen, I thought—and on the other, a sailboat. A strange concept passed through me. Life is like this coin. Contrasting sides. Opposites. One is fixed and doesn't move, like *the face*, and the other is ever flowing, like *the sailboat*, taken by the wind to strange new worlds. It was in that moment that I was made aware that I was having a conscious thought. Up until then, my world had been a series of unconscious reactions to stimuli, with not too much thought or care.

But now, I found myself thinking about polarities; push pull, plus minus, yes no, black white, in out, up down, life death. As I flipped the coin over in my hand, I understood that, although the two sides of the coin were different, they were in fact part of the same whole.

I reasoned with myself that just because a face was on one side, and a boat on the other, that did not mean the two sides were separate; they just looked different. Each part is the whole and each whole is the part. I did not understand the spiritual significance of my thoughts, but the concept stayed with me.

Awareness puts wind in your sails. Without it, the sea remains calm and new lands afar. Awareness brings our human perception to life and shows us what we need to see in order to conduct our lives free from emotional pain and suffering. It's a conscious muscle one can build, and it's catnip for attracting exactly what we want into our lives.

In short, awareness is the golden ticket. *La totale.* Why? Because emotional awareness will enable you to identify your unconscious behaviours. At the age of eight, I had quite unexpectedly had awareness blow into my sails, and my consciousness was teased to awaken.

I'd settled into my new routine and family life. My sister and I fought like regular siblings, and I took immense pleasure in annoying her by singing all the time. In all my happiness, I'd become a songbird. My parents used my chanting to gauge my degree of well-being. The more I sang, the happier it meant I was.

Unfortunately, in 1980, at the age of nine, my cheerful jingles came to a halt. We moved to a little yellow country on the world map no bigger than Lake Ontario called Luxembourg, and my heavenly world of granola-baking stability came crumbling down.

My dad worked in the northern part, Ardennes, and the only English-language school nearby was in Luxembourg, in the southern part. My parents decided to put my sister and me in a boarding school, instead of having my father commute to work every day. The problem was that the boarding school only accepted children thirteen years or older. They felt that separating a young child from her parents before the age of thirteen was not wise. I was nine, turning ten, at the time. My parents overlooked that prudent reasoning and struck up a deal with the school, one that was based on logic and convenience.

In the end, the school allowed it because my older sister, who was then thirteen, would be there and could act as a motherly influence on me. My sister was in actuality a teenager with raging hormones, and her concerns and attention were appropriately focused on other things.

My adoption had only been seven years prior, and for all intents and purposes, I was still in recovery. This separation from my *second* mother felt like another abandonment to me, and that's when the music stopped. Completely. And as the music faded, so did my conscious, joyful connection with my higher self. I began to feel like a mermaid out of water.

There was one boarding house for girls and one boarding house for boys, but for dinner, we would go across the street to the boys' house and eat together. This was not a small village road, but a four-lane street that extended from a highway. The traffic was usually on-and-off heavy, and the cars travelled at high speeds. I had been told by several adults, multiple times, to walk down a block and cross at the lights. On school days, this made sense to me because the school was down by the lights, but for dinner, it seemed like a waste of time to walk *all* the way down to the lights and then back up, just to have a meal. One block is *so far* when you're young and lazy.

On this particular evening, sunlight was a fading friend, and twilight began to create a gloomy mood. There was a sweet smell of rain in the air, brewing somewhere in the distance. I stood with my toes on the curb and waited. When I thought no one was watching, I quickly crossed the first two lanes. I stood stock-still in the middle. Transfixed. Anchored. Waiting. I realised I had misjudged the velocity of the cars coming from the right, because now there were two lanes of traffic on either side of me travelling at very high speeds.

What happened next was quick, and yet slow, at the same time. A car in the far lane decided to pass the car in front of it and was suddenly barreling down at me at 140 clicks an hour. In a split second, there was fear, the word *shit* exploded into my thoughts, and then quick acceptance—I was going to die. I remember knowing that the brakes were not being applied. Then a strange sensation came over me; I was expanding into a vibrational field, stretched and split, if you will, like the mom in the animated movie *The Incredibles*. I was suddenly standing on the other side of the road, looking back at the cars whooshing by. The whole entire human piece of me.

I felt a presence standing there with me. I was not alone. The cars continued to swish by in real time. My thoughts were in a million fractals. The driver never braked. He never saw me, because I wasn't there. I wasn't over there in the middle of the road. I was here. Somehow. Here. My heart was racing, and a voice spoke to me telepathically: *Not today.* I turned towards the boys' boarding house and ran in for dinner.

I'm convinced that science fiction writers have actually experienced the things they write about, whether through space-time transcendence or through the realms of the mind. I believe that's how we co-create the world we live in—by thinking and imaging it into being.

At the age of eleven, I chose to cross a road that brought me an experience that shifted my awareness and perception dramatically. It placed me on a trajectory far outside the realms of what was deemed *normal*.

Most importantly, I knew I was not alone, ever.

Inter-Dimensional Reality

Following this event, I started waking during the night at the exact same time, 4:52 a.m. The red digital rods pulsated in the dark with unnerving repetition. And there, sprawled across my bed and down onto my bedroom floor, was a world of little people. Talking and trading, the hustle and bustle of a miniature world sometime before electricity. I watched them go about their business, afraid to move for fear that my giant body might crush them.

Then one night I awoke at the usual strike of 4:52 a.m., but this time there was no small-scale society sharing my bed. Instead, I was drawn to go to my bedroom window. I moved the thick, cotton curtains to the side and looked out onto the empty street. A male figure was casually leaning against a street-lamp dressed like Dick Tracy from the 1930s comic strip. His long trench coat was yellow and matched his hat. He tipped his hat and looked straight at me. A sudden and strange thought crossed my mind: *The search has begun.* I quickly withdrew from the window and scurried back to the safety of my bed. I prayed for *insta-sleep* and it was granted.

I had no vocabulary for what was happening; it simply became a part of my life. A secret part I was too afraid to share with anyone, for fear of teasing, or worse, being called crazy.

My personal perspective is that we always have assistance from higher dimensional energies, but it comes down to belief. If you don't believe in such things, then you are not likely to ask for assistance, and therefore, not likely to choose to have the awareness. However, once something is in your awareness, it becomes a part of you, absorbed into your cellular experience on a quantum level. The more experiences like this you have, the easier it becomes to have more, until it's as natural as breathing. Other dimensions of reality are simply in the next room; all you have to do is open the door.

Two years later, when I was thirteen, we moved to the city of Munich, in what was, at the time, West Germany. I finally lived at home again and speedily buried the trauma of separation and abandonment deep down in my emotional ocean. At my new school, I found my connection again. This time with a girl named Melissa. She was also intrigued by metaphysics and all things esoteric. We shared experiences and talked for hours on the phone, testing each other's ability to use our third eye to foresee things. She would hold a playing card in her hand somewhere on the other side of the city, and I would have to guess the card by focusing my attention inward. We took turns, and after a few weeks, it became obvious that I had a bit of a knack for this game. Sadly, when Melissa moved abroad, I had no more friends to share these pastimes with, and my focus became sports and academics.

During the next three years, I was thriving with a capital T. I flourished in sports, academics, and the arts. I directed and acted in a production of *The Rocky Horror Picture Show* and won the talent show. I received the science award in the eighth grade, and I broke records for high jump and track. I was MVP for girls' basketball two years in a row and practiced on the varsity boys' team. I was aglow, brightly beaming, and in the *zone*. I was connected with my higher self, and utterly shocked a few months later when my inner fire was all but snuffed out.

CHAPTER TWO

1989–1999

"Once you label me, you negate me."

—Søren Kierkegaard

When I was in the tenth grade, we moved again. This time to Marseille, France. My mom was born and raised in Edmonton, Alberta, commonly referred to as "Deadmonton," so this city on the French Riviera, with all its culture and pizazz, was a dream come true for her. Unfortunately, my parents forgot to look at the broader picture of why things had gone so well for me at my previous school—the sports and arts programmes—and instead enrolled me in an academically prestigious French school, where I was to do a bilingual international baccalaureate. I was to go to school Monday through Saturday and would not be able to participate in any athletic programmes because they didn't offer any.

I know my parents' intentions were good, just misguided. I think the end game was that this opportunity would guarantee me a spot at university pretty much anywhere in the world. My mom might have also secretly been swayed to enroll me in this highly acclaimed school because of how it would reflect on her. I imagine she played out the future conversations with diplomats' wives and curious neighbours. Having a child who was attending one of the most prestigious schools in France was way better than wearing a Chanel suit or Hermès scarf.

What no one had anticipated was that this highly sought-after school promoted discouragement of its students. The French schools held this horrendous event once a semester called *conseil de classe*. It was a gathering of the entire grade together with the headmaster and dean of students in which each student was called upon and told how worthless they were. Even the best, most studious student in our grade was quite pathetic, according to the headmaster. Maybe other schools managed their *conseil de classe* in a more humane way, but this school did not.

To the French kids, this was sort of normal, as they had grown up with this system, and I'm guessing they'd grown a thick skin in response to the stinging words of discouragement. But to me, a young, developing woman who had been encouraged and even praised for being good at school, for being creative, and showered with accolades for her athletic prowess, this conduct by the headmaster and dean of students was an utter shock. As much as we students would joke about how meaningless and awful these sessions were, the harsh words of negativity began to awaken a deeply rooted fear within me.

In reaction to this, and the non-creative, non-athletic school setting, I began to fall out of love with myself and to act out. It was just small things at first, but the more out of resonance with myself I became, and the more I was forced into this world of external conditions and expectations, the more I rebelled.

Young love and schoolwork, most definitely in that order, became all-encompassing. As a teenager living in a large city, I was out at night exploring with friends and not always completely sober. I remember hearing a loud voice in my head one particular night that beckoned me to take a "*taxi*" home. There was an urgency to it, so I obeyed. Taxis were expensive, and I was teenage-poor, so the metro was my chosen mode of transportation. However, late at night, the metro was a petri dish crawling with no shortage of wankers and weirdos, so I spent the last of my money on a cab and got home in ten minutes flat. I'm not sure what might have happened if I'd taken the subway home that night, but the voice seemed to keep me out of harm's way more than once.

My first love was a deliciously handsome and intelligent young man from Canada. Part Brazilian, part Italian, part Indian, part incredible. A slender boy full of life, wit, intelligence, enthusiasm, and thank goodness, an equal amount of teenage infatuation for me. His name was Sam, which would become somewhat of a trend with men and me.

Like all young love, our passion and affection were nervous and intense. When he moved back to Canada, we were both devastated. Broken dreams and shredded hearts. We wrote letters to one another and tried to maintain a relationship, but it was 1988 and we were still in the dark ages—no internet. No texting. No video chatting. One letter would take two weeks to arrive at its destination, and I was constantly getting in trouble for the scandalous long-distance phone bills. My oh my, how times have changed.

I made a conscious choice months later that would redirect my life considerably. I chose to date another young man who also lived in another country but was at least on the same continent. This was one of the first times I made a decision based on my logical mind, and not my heart. My inner being yearned for my first love, and I wish I'd had the emotional smarts to know how to make "us" work back then, but sadly, I did not. I broke his heart and dated this other young man based on false charm and proximity. I let my rational mind take the lead. I had fallen out of the sweet, resonant zone with my Higher Self.

Much to Unlearn

One can adapt to almost anything, and Mom and Dad's quarreling simply became background noise. Their dysfunctional dynamic was stuck on repeat and played over and over. I could always escape to the quiet of my room and shut the racket out. My motto became–*if you can't solve it, avoid it!*

It was quite obvious that my dad's explosive temper seemed to correlate with stress, which led to drinking, which contributed to poor judgement. He always had a way of ruining my joyful spirit and cutting me down to size. As I blossomed into a young woman, the vibrational frequency and energy I exuded were those of spontaneous adventure, fierce independence, and curiosity for life. I think the plumage of my feathers was like an allergen to him, or maybe he simply yearned for some peace and consistency. I was in a constant state of wonder and untainted excitement. Everything I did was too passionate. I was a teenager and wild child after all, wasn't that my "job"? Similar to the archetype of the trickster in "Goldilocks and the Three Bears," I had no regard for rules and what I was "*meant*" to do.

How do you please the unpleasable person? I learned when I was a teenager that you don't. All you can do is follow your own passion and purpose. It's the only way to begin to feel better when you feel deflated or misunderstood. I didn't have fancy terms for what was going on, but my awareness was active enough by then to know what I didn't want.

On my eighteenth birthday, we went out for dinner to my favourite Thai restaurant. By dessert, my Dad had absorbed two Scotches, almost an entire bottle of wine, and was moving in on the Cognac. His ability to govern his emotions was numbed by drink, and I'd come to learn that it was best to avoid him under those conditions. But I was blindsided on many occasions simply because I was in my happy place and not consciously aware that I needed to be alert. That was the case on my eighteenth birthday.

It was a big occasion, and I had every reason to be fired up. When the dessert menu arrived, I bubbled over in delight and eagerly teased about getting two. My father gave me a swift kick under the table with his hard-tipped leather shoe. It tore my stocking and the pain ripped through my cheerful spirit. He stared my enthusiasm into the table and told me to *be careful*.

I looked out the window and wondered why he felt compelled to rob me of my joy, of my beauty, of myself.

I refused to eat dessert that night and consciously chose never to sit across from him at a table ever again. Turning eighteen was tainted with a blow to my spirited zest. And so, on my eighteenth birthday, the real gift I received that night was the gift of contrast. It was a clarifying moment wherein my desire to be independent and free was launched. I now had a newfound mission—tack my sails the minute the wind turned in my favour and walk tall in my own lane and power one day. In that knowing came a wave of relief and a true sense of purpose and empowerment. I turned to these words of Ralph Waldo Emerson many times when I was in doubt: "Do not go where the path may lead, go instead where there is no path and leave a trail."

It was during those teenage years that I was taken back to that dime, and my first awareness of polarities. Same coin of life, same coin of family, but my dad and I were on opposite sides of it. My side was an open ocean, while his was the stiff profile of a monarch. He thought. I felt. He was logical. I was emotional. He sought knowledge. I sought wisdom. His motto was, "Work hard and you'll be successful." My motto was, "Follow your passion and you'll be fulfilled." He had no ability to understand me because I was like nothing in his learned repertoire of how things should be. His box of unconscious conditions and beliefs were screaming, *"You must obey me! Do as I say, it's the only way!"*

I was nineteen the last time I had a physical encounter with my dad. He hit me with a fire log for calling out to my sister in the stairwell. I stormed into my room and slammed the door. Later that evening, I dug deep into my bag of bravery and delivered this line to him: "If you ever lay a hand on me again, or threaten me physically, I will go to the police. I will press charges." The gist of my words permeated his being for what seemed an eternity. There was never a meeting of eyes or an apology, just a simple and affirmative, "Understood."[1]

Siddhartha

My favourite book when I was a teenager was *Siddhartha* by Hermann Hesse. It's not much of a surprise that I identified so distinctly with the main character. Like Siddhartha, I was expected to follow in my dad's footsteps. And in a similar way to Siddhartha, at some moment in time I realised that my parents had attained a certain level of wealth and knowledge, but not wisdom and enlightenment. Fortunately, my first love's father, Terence, had a similar curiosity for the unknowable, and we spent many afternoons glimpsing at the possibility of a transcendent power, a higher truth, and musing over whether there was more to this nutty world than met the eye. These

---

[1] In that moment, I instantly learned your voice is one of your most powerful tools. As children, we forget that we have rights. Moms and dads, uncles and aunts, become idolized like gods. Just remember, they're human, too, and make bad decisions and take wrong turns just as you do. There is always help, always a way out, and you do have rights. Your parents have no right to humiliate, gaslight, or physically harm you. Never be afraid to seek help or counsel. You have every right to be treated fairly and live in an environment that is safe, one that allows you to grow to your potential. These rights are listed in the UN Convention on the Rights of the Child, something I recommend every parent read for themselves and share with their children.

conversations and communion with Terence always made me feel seen and witnessed, cherished and perceived. That was the gift of my rapport with Terence. It is marvelous to be appreciated and valued—is it not what we live for? There is nothing quite like it.

This line in *Siddhartha* resonated with me so powerfully: "It is not for me to judge another man's life. I must judge, I must choose, I must spurn, purely for myself. For myself, alone." These words inspired and motivated me to follow my own path.

So often, parents give us a road map we can use, and then mostly get in the way. Instead of allowing us to determine our own lane, they tell us we need to take the highway, it's faster and safer, and the scenic route is riddled with unknowns.

But that is just their own external conditioning coming through them.

External conditioning and social constructs are what trip so many of us up. So often kids are taught *what* to think, not *how* to think. The cultural conditioning of today, or the box of limiting beliefs, disallows for alignment with your higher consciousness. In my view, if conditioning were a punishable crime, it would get a life sentence. It creates zombies out of people and then puts them on death row—they're dead before they're dead. Considering the complexity of our Universe and the conspiracy of thought and desire that go into bringing us here, it seems like a damn shame to have it all go amuck because of some external forces and false expectations. It is my firm belief that the latter is what creates a disconnect from our inner power and true calling.

My own life is a great example of continual battles with conditioning. I grew up in an atheist household, one that was open to all cultures and creeds, but considerably conservative when it came to the life path I was expected to follow. My dad immigrated to Canada from Hungary with his family when he was thirteen and learned through his own external conditioning that if you worked hard, did well in school, and went to university, then you would have opportunities to make something of yourself—a commonly shared viewpoint by the Baby Boomer generation and one that undoubtedly brought that generation success and wealth. However, their education and upbringing defined them, I believe, to the point where they could not, and were indeed frightened to, look outside their limiting conditions and beliefs.

The post-WWII idea of a nine-to-five job being the only way to succeed was hardwired into the operating systems of the Baby Boomer's and passed on to their kids. And just like that, what you believe is who you are.

University

My desire to study acting and filmmaking was not taken seriously by my parents. It was not something they considered desirable or much of a potential moneymaker. Getting a degree and a nine-to-five was much more aligned with what they understood as a path to success. At the age of nineteen, and thoroughly against my wishes, I was forced to attend university in Canada. I went from one academic prison to another, and the freedom I craved and my desire to pursue my passion and dreams continued to elude me.

I arrived in Montreal during the humid days of late August, already counting the weeks until I was free to leave. My Soul-self was eager to get on the right track. Having been raised in Europe, I felt very out of place in this North American setting. The weeks went by like winter's molasses. The more trapped I felt, the more of a surge I had to break free. All options were on the table. I finally decided on a plan of action that I knew was not wise but would buy me a plane ticket to freedom. I decided to steal $600 from a friend and buy a one-way ticket to Europe to follow my passion of pursuing a career in film. I know, I hear ya, worst plan ever. Well, I did it anyway and sat rather numbly one afternoon on my dorm bed with $600 in my hands thinking, *What have I done?*

I was so guilt-ridden I didn't sleep for thirty-six hours. Finally, I changed my dumb plan to an even dumber plan. I decided to give the money back. Discreetly. Which I did. But this act only triggered the head of residence to call the police, and the entire residence was combed. Everyone was a suspect. My guilt got the better of me, and, after chewing off a few fingernails, I fessed up, naïvely hoping that my confession would make the big mess I'd created go away.

The operative words here are "…*big mess* I'd *created*…" I was finally free and off the restricted island of home and parents. I could do things differently, and yet, within five months of this new beginning, I had simply created another limited island to live on.

I was rebelling against the fact that my voice had not been respected and listened to, that I was not allowed to follow my dreams. Yet, instead of just getting through it quietly, I unconsciously chose to kick up a storm and let everyone know how unhappy I was. The only problem was that no one understood my unconscious behaviours for what they truly were, least of all me, and I was treated like the criminal I'd chosen to become. I'd constructed yet another setting where people did not understand or embrace me, and my cycle of abandonment was spinning out of control like a helicopter without a tail rotor.

This familiar conditioned trauma was all about the patterns in my life up to that point. My original wound dated back to my first few years of life and directly correlated to not feeling unconditionally loved, accepted, or cherished. Unconsciously, I was reshaping new scenarios all the time that matched that vibrational reality.

The dean of students called my lost friend, the victim, and me in for a meeting with the police detective. It was declared that I would be able to live in residence until the end of the year (five more months), but after that, it was strictly forbidden. I wept and begged for forgiveness, apologizing profusely as I tried to explain why I had acted so irrationally. But naturally, there was no sympathy airborne in that room; these people did not know me, nor did they care to know me now.

It was also stated that this matter should remain between the people present in the dean's office, so as to avoid unnecessary scandal and gossip. But that bargain was not kept by my lost friend, and the news of my conduct spread like wildfire.

Though no charges were pressed, the girls in the dorm decided that a good ol'-fashioned Dark Ages penance of "public shaming" was the best way to discipline me. I had never been a thief before and had no idea how to receive the onslaught of immediate and relentless shaming. For five months, every time I walked into a room, everyone got up and left. If I walked on the same sidewalk as other students, everyone evaporated like fog in the sun. Every evening, thirty or so students sitting at the long wooden dining table would promptly rise and leave the minute one of the shame hounds sniffed me out. If I asked someone a question, they'd either glare at me in scornful silence or reply swiftly with, "Did I hear something?" and walk away like I didn't exist. *But who could blame them?*

I finally gave up eating altogether and decided that smoking was way less humiliating than going for a meal, and about the same price as a shawarma at Ali Baba's. I avoided the common room, classes, people, and pretty much timed my comings and goings around when I was most likely not to run into any freshman girls from my dorm.

My roommate was my only friend. She had a different perspective—we all make mistakes—and she felt that giving the money back, confessing, and forgoing the residence was penance enough for such a petty crime. She said that the shaming the girls were taking such pleasure in was simply a sign of their petty-minded, mean-spirited, faltering integrities. Like the bully, it made them feel powerful, when in fact they had very little strength of character at all.

However, this was all on me. I had not remained authentic to my true self, and I'd quickly put the record of neglect and shame on repeat. All I really longed for was love and acceptance and to be able to follow my own path. I craved true freedom. I wanted to quench the thirst of my Soul. *Why was that so hard?*

Marseille • NY • Copenhagen

In June, I moved back to Marseille and buried my university experiences in a virtual graveyard. I lived at home again, which was not ideal for me *or* my parents, but I didn't earn enough to be able to pay rent yet. I'd been accepted at a bilingual acting studio affiliated with The Actors Studio in New York. In the end, my parents paid for my acting classes, and after the first year, the school gave me a scholarship to study in New York for half a year.

New York was an adventure, and I wasn't unlawfully disconnected to my Higher Self the entire time I was there. Progress. I got private voice lessons from a well-known voice coach who had me singing scales to I-love-my-dawg-a-awg, and I trained in dance and body movement at The Ailey Studios. Living arrangements were not covered, so I crashed on the couch of my friend's brother's roach-infested flat. Every night, I tucked myself in tight like a tamale so no roaches could spoon me. As soon as I turned the lights out, I could hear their little feet scuttle across the linoleum floor. All said and done, I didn't sleep much.

After that year, I returned to Marseille and got an agent.

Following umpteen casting calls and more rejections than I care to share, my agent finally succeeded in getting me a part in a Mike Figgis movie called *Women & Men 2*. I played the super-glamourous role of a young Parisienne prostitute, strutting my stuff in fishnet stockings and pleather miniskirt across the slick, wet pavement, and delivered one short line.

My career as an actress might not have launched me into stardom as I'd hoped, but that night I discovered another role, one that had me totally captivated. That of the director. I watched Mike Figgis as he directed his actors, and I was suddenly struck with the knowing—*that* was what I wanted to do.

I watched as he spoke with his camera crew about framing. They rehearsed the dolly movement back and forth several times to get it just right. He walked the principal actor through his movements and praised him for doing a fantastic job. I was turning blue in my next-to-naked wardrobe, but I wanted to digest every bit of knowledge from what was to be my very first film class.

During those all-too-few days on set, I stayed in the shadows, but in earshot of Figgis and his crew. I observed the intricate machinery of filmmaking and studied all its moving parts. Figgis was very personable, and he made everyone feel like their contribution to the film was the most important part.

As soon as I was done, I dove headfirst into researching film schools and quickly discovered that, to get accepted to a film school in France, you had to make a movie first. *C'est what? Wasn't that the whole point of going to film school? To learn how to make a movie?* The year was 1991, and we didn't have digital cameras or iPhones. Sure, most people had thrown out their rabbit-ear antennas, but just to set the tone, cell phones weighed about four kilograms and took ten hours to charge. We were at the very early stages of transitioning from analogue to digital, but not quite there yet. Film equipment was outrageously expensive. I quickly concluded that film schools in France were out of the question.

My boyfriend at the time was living in Gothenburg, Sweden, and so I researched schools there. I didn't speak a word of Swedish, but languages can be learned, right? I went ahead and applied. During my interview, the head of school asked me the very logical question: "How are you going to follow the classes if you don't speak Swedish?" I matter-of-factly told him I already had three languages swimming around in my brain and was confident there was room for a fourth. He simply responded, "If you think you can do it, then I'll give you the opportunity to at least try." One ginormous suitcase and a javelin-sized Tunisian carpet were all the possessions I needed for my fresh new start.

New Days, Old Ways

Unfortunately, I had yet to identify my unconscious conditioning blueprint that was still on repeat, and my boyfriend rapidly became my project, not my partner. He, too, was no stranger to shame. I wanted to help him, cure him, save him. I truly believed I could, but the part that eluded me was that I had yet to save myself. I had yet to understand my own unconscious archetype at play, and I did not yet value myself, my worth, or my own growth.

He cheated on me and lied constantly and then turned around and loved and protected me. It was a vicious, confusing cycle, one that was so similar to my conditioning up until that point. We shared a Bonnie and Clyde bond of *us against the world*, and he played the *no-one-understands-you-but-me* card constantly. After a while, I began to believe that I couldn't do anything without him. It was a recognizable song, so I sang along. It was what I knew, and in an unhealthy way, it was my *normal* and what I thought I wanted and deserved. The Fleetwood Mac song "Dreams" warned me time and time again with the lyrics *"...players only love you when they're playing..."* but I wasn't conscious enough to hear the meaning.

Here I was, miles away from home on my new ride called *freedom*, yet the only gears it had were *worthless* and *underserving*. I switched between these all throughout that detrimental relationship until another man showed up and began to shine a light on my inner sprockets of kindness, wholeness, and beauty.

This new man was my saving grace. By loving me unconditionally, he slowly began to help me see myself for who I truly was. Mr. True Love was a beautiful reflection of love, tenderness, and generosity. I often got scared because I didn't know how to act around his love and vulnerability. He never understood why I avoided him after a night of passionate togetherness. I didn't have the awareness to explain it to him, but his love freaked me out. It was not my MO, and I really struggled with how to just let it wash me clean.

Through my circumstances, I'd been taught that love was neglectful, occasionally abusive, and certainly had expectations. So when true love walked into my room, I didn't recognise it for what it was. It might as well have been a visitor from a distant galaxy. When he asked me to marry him, instead of jumping into his arms with a delighted *"I do I do!"* I started peddling the other way on my bike of shame. *Why would he want to marry me?* I had not yet learned for myself what my value was, and so instead of leaping into his arms crazy with love, I flip-flopped like a fish out of water for two years. By the time I was ready to commit, he had moved on to other shores. He wrote me a note once that read: *Take care of yourself now. Remember, you are a beautiful woman. 9.8 on a scale of 10. I have not proposed to you for the last time. Just so you know.* I cherished those words for years and reverted back to them whenever I felt unloved or unworthy.

Relinquishing Control

When I was in my last semester of film school, I produced and directed a low-budget music video for an up-and-coming band. It aired on ZTV (the Swedish version of MTV) and was well received. One day, out of the blue, I received a phone call from a producer who had seen my music video asking me if I'd be interested in working for her company as a commercial director. I was still in school and satiating my wolf's appetite with curry rice and gourmet instant noodle soups. *A job? A paying job?* I agreed to a meeting and was hired on the spot. This opportunity had very little to do with my conscious control, it simply flowed to me. I had not participated in creating this opportunity in any way except that I was following my passion and allowing for opportunities to enter my sphere. I was in my sweet, resonant zone, and my barricades of resistance were down. I was simply open to receiving whatever came my way. The more I did this, the more the path of potential opened to me.

A year later, one of my dearest friends introduced me to the book *Women Who Run with the Wolves* by Clarissa Pinkola Estés. She let me borrow her very worn edition and soon thereafter gifted me my own copy. I immediately began to underline and highlight passages that resonated with me. I devoured this book in its entirety and then immediately started over. It marked the beginning of a journey, one that would reward me with one of my greatest gifts—Soul reclamation. *Women Who Run with the Wolves* helped me to begin understanding my true nature and shifted my perspective on many levels. What I'd been fighting was in fact my conditioning and socialization. Up until this point, I'd challenged my family and educational institutions without truly understanding why I was feuding. It was purely instinctual. My inner wild woman craved freedom to create, and longed to make life her own. She was my inner strength

25

and resilience when the world tried to break my spirit. My wild woman longed for passion, creative madness—and love.

A few months later, at the annual advertising awards in Cannes, I met a female producer on the beach. I recognised her familiar Canadian accent, and we struck up a conversation. She invited me to send her my demo reel, as she was looking to build her roster of directors in Vancouver. When I returned home to Gothenburg, I sent her my reel, and two weeks later, she made me an offer too good to be true. A gust of luck had blown through my door.

At this point, I was in my late twenties, and my wild woman was clawing to be released. I'd been working for the same production company for more than five years, and moving on had definitely crossed my mind. I sat looking out over the expanse of the Gothenburg canals from my fourth-floor apartment while lyrics from The Clash played over and over in my head: *"Should I stay or should I go?"*

That night, I awoke in the darkness, and for all I know it might very well have been 4:52 a.m., but it was 1998 and I didn't have an iPhone to tell me the time. My Spirit guide Dick Tracy stood in my kitchen, with the familiar casual lean I remembered so vividly from when I was ten. I was startled by the "realness" of him, and my heart began to race. Before I could react, I was launched into a vision. I was suddenly standing on the railing of my fourth-floor apartment, barefoot and unsteady. I swiveled my head back and saw Dick Tracy walking towards me, calmly gesturing for me to jump. I turned back and panicked at the thought of plunging to my death. Suddenly, I heard a voice. *"Jump and you will soar. Eighteen years it will take."* And before I could react, I'd jumped off the railing and shape-shifted into a white eagle. The feeling of freedom was so sweet. I glided fancy-free upon my feathery wings, liberated. Needless to say, I accepted the job offer and moved to Vancouver four weeks later.

CHAPTER THREE

1999–2008

"It takes courage to grow up and become who you are."

—E. E. Cummings

I moved to Vancouver and, ironically, my producer found me an apartment in a house on the same block as my first love, Sam. *What were the odds? Was the spark still there?* Absolutely. But we were both struggling to find our way in the world, and our potential love hung on the wall like a crooked painting. He found a girlfriend shortly after I arrived, and she helped find me a roomie—I needed assistance paying the rent.

Sam #2 arrived one Sunday morning to see the place. I was apprehensive about sharing with a man I didn't know, but he was a Buddhist, Gauloise-smoking social worker. *How unhinged could he be?* Sam #2 became my roommate and lifelong friend.

Many a night were spent discussing Buddhism in a cloud of no-filter Gauloise haze, and S2 introduced me to the concept of the bodhisattva, a person who is working towards his own liberation, towards enlightenment. I was engrossed in his every word and asked questions like a curious child. My awareness had been sparked, and I began an unconscious process of seeking my own path of enlightenment.

A shift in awareness can happen in anybody at any time. A lot of the time, it's a cataclysmic event, like a death of a loved one, the birth of a baby, divorce, an unfaithful partner, a despairing depression or diagnosis—some God-awful-out-of-this-world-mind-blowing event that makes you want to either crawl up and die, or scream a joyful hallelujah from the treetops. It's an event that shifts your point of perspective. I was about to undergo three major shifts, and many minor ones, all of which would contribute in some way to my new perception of this illusory reality.

First Shift

I'd been searching for several years and found out that my biological mother had died when I was fifteen years old. I secretly wondered what I had been doing the day she died. *Did I have any inkling of her passing? Did she come visit me in Spirit before heading home?* If she did, I had no recollection of it whatsoever.

She also took the secret of who my biological father was with her to the great beyond. As I began hunting for my biological father using traditional methods of investigation, I realised my search was utterly futile. I decided to explore options beyond my box of *normal*. I contacted a psychic medium in the sunny state of California, who had been recommended to me by a friend. *What did I have to lose?* Eighty bucks was all.

My one-hour reading with this cheery woman left me completely speechless. She described the room in which I was sitting in great detail; she even related the fact that I was speaking on a cordless phone and not on a landline phone, and could I please call her back from the landline! I scanned my room for hidden cameras and looked to the sky for passing satellites. She recounted people, places, and events from my deceased mother's life at length. I scribbled notes furiously in hopes that this information from the beyond would somehow guide me to my biological father.

I hung up completely bewildered. *How was this possible?* My interdimensional experiences as a young girl were not dissimilar, yet it had been a long time since my awareness had been tickled by other worlds and such nuance. I knew what the psychic had done was possible because I had just witnessed it for myself, but my mind ran the track of rational logic a couple hundred times, trying to decode the *how*.

During the next week, I began to recognise that there was something rather grand going on that I'd been missing all these years. My curiosity was ablaze, and I suddenly found myself wondering, *What else is eluding me?* This one psychic reading alone had shifted my awareness enough to lead me on a new road of truth-seeking. I kicked down the door of my numbed consciousness and peered out the other side. I had a yearning to understand how this was possible and maybe even to acquire these skills for myself.

The Merry Medium

I took the information I'd received from the first medium and shared it with my godmother, Joyce, the first living friend of my mother's I had found. She confirmed the accuracy of the details, and she, too, was stunned at the prospect that it was possible to reach into the ethers with your mind and retrieve information.

Seeing as the first reading had been such a success, I decided to find a local medium to work with, to help me on my continuing quest. I browsed the internet and found a website with a mauve colour scheme and instantly felt drawn to the picture of the woman. Her name was Martina and her working name was "The Merry Medium." *What was not to like?* I booked a reading and met her a few days later.

Over the course of the following nine months, I took the information from my readings with Martina and began piecing together a Hockney-esque, fractured portrait of my biological father. I learned that he had acne scars on his face; that he knew of my existence but had not participated in raising me; had at least three other children from another woman, all older than me; had lived in New Mexico; and was either living or buried near a quaint, white church somewhere in Ontario, specific location unknown. Every time I got a new piece of information from Martina, I would hand it over to Joyce and eagerly wait to see if she could finally identify who he was. One piece of information that came up over and over was that his name was on a card or piece of paper that was currently hidden from sight (super useful, right?) and that, when it was found, it would reveal who my biological father was.

I did a guided meditation with Martina with the intention of meeting my biological father "in Spirit," and the only thing to show up to meet me was a German Shepherd with very pointed ears. I was told this was how his energy had decided to show up: distant and none too eager to talk.

The whole endeavour was tiresome and dragged on for several years. Yet my determined character kept plowing forward. Finally, I broke it down to the nitty gritty—to the weekend I was conceived. I simply asked Joyce to tell me which men had been in my mother's life at that time. *It really had to be that simple!* Joyce jogged down memory lane with me over and over until one day Martina told me that I had to let go of the outcome and then it would reveal itself. I hated advice like that. It meant you got your wish when you didn't desperately want it anymore. *What was the fun in that?*

But it was my first lesson in surrender. Releasing any attachment to any outcome is the best way to manifest it. Easier said than done, seeing as we want what we want when we want it. But I finally collected my copious amounts of scribbled research and stashed it all away for a rainy day. I choked out a tear or two and accepted I would never know who my biological father was. Like a king in check, I had no more moves.

Chile

In 2000, I went to Chile to direct a few commercials. Work had been slow in Canada and a director friend told me there was plenty of opportunity in Santiago. I didn't speak Spanish, but heck, languages can be learned, right? So when an offer to shoot three commercials came in, I accepted without hesitation. A week later, I flew down to Chile's capital, a city sprawl surrounded by the snow-capped Andes mountains.

The executive producer met me at the airport and drove me to my quaint hotel. It was obvious that communicating was going to be a bit of a challenge; his English was rudimentary, and my Spanish was nonexistent. I used French as a base and then just made words up by adding *a* to the end. It sounded like Spanish to me. He just looked at me blankly and smiled. *"No te preocupes."* His response and solution to most things. Loosely translated, it means, "Don't worry about it."

We worked it out with hand gestures and a lot of laughs. He showed me DOP (director of photography) reels, one after the other. They all had the same slick, lit look and they didn't much appeal to me. My poor producer began looking outside his box of options. Time was of the essence, and we considered flying someone in from the US. Then, one afternoon, he showed me the reel of a young, inexperienced photographer. I watched what was basically a film school reel and was immediately impressed. I liked that this young DOP was not afraid of dark spaces and shadows, and he definitely did not overlight. I could see his budding talent, and I knew we'd found our guy. My producer was hesitantly delighted.

Enter stage right, Sam #3. It was humorous, but I inwardly wondered if it had a deeper meaning. *Why so many Sams?* On day three of our shoot, I found myself falling for S3 quite unexpectedly. I'd always been very professional while working and never crossed that line, but something about this young man sucked me in like water to a drain.

Five months later, he and I were living together in Santiago. I told him about my history with Mr. Shame and forewarned him that infidelity and adultery were deal-breakers for me. He understood and proclaimed enduring fidelity.

About a year later, I proposed over cocktails one night, and the next morning, we whisked ourselves off to Vegas and got married at a kitschy Chapel of Love. It was the stuff of cheesy fairy tales and it all happened in a flurry of reckless spontaneity. We were young and erotically stupid. As Patrick Süskind wrote, "According to Plato, fools do not strive for the beautiful and the good, for divine bliss, because they are satisfied with themselves."

Moxie the Wonderdog

July 3, 2001 unfolded in a way I never could have predicted. I'd been working at the office and had a quick lunch with my assistant, Sam #4 no less. We meandered through a park after lunch and passed one homeless dog after the other. He told me about his recent dog rescue; a large crème brûlée–coloured Rhodesian Ridgeback mutt. He was madly in love and named his new companion "Santos." I mentioned how I'd already taken one rather distraught German shepherd hybrid to the vet for treatment and explained how, in the end, Lola had to be put out of her misery as she was too old and frail to fight her numerous ailments. I told S4 how I wished I could take them all home, but unfortunately my allergies were a problem. We crossed at some lights, and right in front of a department store sat three ladies on a bench, eating juicy churrasco sandwiches. Squirming impatiently at their feet, salivating like a crazed cartoon character, was an adorable grey-and-white street dog. S4 pointed at the cute furball. "What about him?" I looked down at the dog, who was utterly fixated on the dripping meat-filled sandwiches. "His fur looks hypoallergenic, maybe part Maltese." "You think he's homeless?" S4 went back and asked the ladies what they knew about the dog. They said he was there every day at noon keenly waiting for his share of their lunch. He confirmed what I suspected; unbelievably, adorable dog needed a forever home.

As we walked away, S4 told me to call the dog to see if he would come. Before I had the chance to ask, *Then what?* I turned towards the cute canine and called out, "Malty!" He instantly perked up, turned towards us, and bolted in our direction. He ran right past us down the street and sprinted up the steps to the entrance of my apartment building. He stared in our direction and barked twice, as if to say, *Hurry up!* S4 and I looked at each other, pleasantly entertained. This pooch had character. We reached the top of the stairs, and I curiously questioned, "Now what?" My friend said he would get his car and take us to the vet.

That is how Malty, whom I named Moxie, for his fiery and spirited nature, came into my life. He has been with me for almost twenty years now, through marriage and divorce, births and deaths, earthquakes and Rottweiler attacks, and a few continental moves. He has been a steady and loyal companion and a fierce protector of both me and my son. When the earthquake cracked the walls of our apartment, Moxie forced me to flee when I froze in panic. When my husband left me, Moxie remained. When my baby slept, Moxie guarded his room with steadfast purpose. When the nights were sleepless, Moxie was my weary-eyed comrade. When the Rottweiler attacked,

Moxie fought the fight I surely would have lost. When spiritual awakening knocked at my door, Moxie kept me sane. When anxiety paralysed me, Moxie was my rock. When my son was old enough to leave home for weeks at a time, Moxie filled my heartache and loneliness with love and play. Moxie was "more man" than any man I'd ever met.

The dog is a true gift, a constant donor, like the sun. Leaps and bounds of pure joy and a wagging tail like the smiles of a friend. The dog's love is playful and steady, telling no lies. She illuminates the way to the way, just like the Tao. The dog is not imprisoned by the Ego—she is a master of compassion and love. She demonstrates effortlessly, day in and day out, the benefits of surrender and allowing. I've been charmed with Moxie medicine and love much longer than the span of the average dog-human bond. Our discovery of one another was auspicious, and I can only hope I've learned a trick or two from my four-legged friend. To summarize, in the words of Franz Kafka: "All knowledge, the totality of all questions and answers, is contained in the dog."

Vision of Hope

In 2004, after being married for three years, when I was thirty-four years old, my first pregnancy ended in a miscarriage at eleven weeks. My baby had not come to stay. A dark cloud of depression hung over me night and day. I lingered in bed, trying to soothe my soul while my husband left for work, unable to be present with my grief. I might have noticed his disconnected Ego and lack of emotional maturity at work had I been more aware at the time, but in those moments, I saw nothing at all.

I was having my very own *Heart of Darkness* moment. I was Colonel Kurtz at the end of the world in my bedroom cave all alone. The only difference was the types of horror we had experienced. It was a lonely place. Moxie kept me warm when the icy winds of solitude blew through my soul. I wondered how I was going to go to work in two days and face my colleagues with no baby in my belly. I drip-dripped like day-old diner coffee. I gazed around my room, looking for answers in the invisible ink on my walls. Then, completely unexpectedly, the most magical thing happened. A beautiful vision appeared at the end of my bed. A hairless girl, or boy, seated like a Buddha, was suspended in glorious hues of orange and yellow rays. I was rendered speechless by the astounding beauty and radiating sense of peace. No art director or painter could ever duplicate such a display of magnificence.

My brain immediately tried to quantify what was happening. I estimated the being to be four or five years old. My inner core suddenly understood that this apparition was not about age or gender. This vision of sublimity just levitated before me in loving patience, waiting for me to receive. As my energy shifted from wanting to quantify the experience to just accepting it, a tsunami of love-filled bliss washed over my entire body. A love I'd never experienced before. Rapture, euphoria didn't quite qualify. It was something beyond that. It was a symphony of visual poetry, an unspoiled, vibrational heaven and a feeling of limitless love beyond human emotions.

I was acutely aware that I wanted to stay in the presence of this apparition forever and ever, basking in its otherworldly ecstasy. Then, the androgynous being spoke to my mind without moving his lips. *"Take care of your body."* This was a direct message to stop smoking because in my darkest moment I found solace in only one thing. The angelic tourist then continued. *"And try again."*

Long. Silent. Pause.

Excuse me? Are you completely out of your Buddha-tastic-blissful mind? And risk going through another miscarriage? Get me a chocolate crepe first, and then we'll talk.

The unprocessed being just looked back at me and flooded me with more love. The vision lingered for a few seconds, as if to make sure I had received the essence of the message. I soaked up every ounce of blessedness from this vision and silently begged for it to take me with it. I wanted to go to that place of orangey yellow light. I wanted to bathe in its rapture of ecstasy and love. *Could we maybe jar it and bring it back to Earth? Drink it for breakfast and sell it as special sauce?*

And then, in the blink of an eye, it was gone.

The darkness returned. I stared at what was now a blank wall, wide-eyed and stupefied. But I felt immensely lighter. And then quite suddenly, I felt a glimmer of hope stir within me. *"Try again."* In that moment, I just *knew* my next pregnancy would be fine and I would carry my baby to term. A major shift had occurred within me. My perspective had changed. I dropped the depression bricks and began to put my misplaced pieces back together. I went down to the kitchen and made myself a chocolate crepe.

Two months later, I was pregnant for the second time. My husband was very happy with the new baby news. He was very candid and had stated openly that having kids was the next obvious stage for us, and that if we didn't have any, then what was the point of partnership? Maybe I should have left at that point, but then a damaged part of myself decided to agree with him. Not in a way that I was aware of at the time, but in a self-love deficit kind of way. It whispered in an all too familiar, haunting voice, *"If you don't give him what he wants, he will leave you. You dig?"* My codependency and early childhood conditioning were still alive and well.

Thankfully, I had the best pregnancy ever. I felt amazing, did yoga, and finally had bloggable boobs. Only my husband was away for most of it. Off somewhere shooting a film that would launch him into Oscar-winning stardom. *"You're pregnant, not sick!"* is a line I'll never forget.

I was aware that something was amiss, but because I was pregnant, I couldn't fathom the idea of having a child alone, even though I was alone all the time anyway. But that sliver of a tether that attached me to the father of my unborn child gave me a sense of hope.

Surrender

With my Soul-self back in a semi-coma and my baby about to be born, I went into nesting mode and prepared the house a million times over for the arrival of our child. Life was literally on hold. Nothing mattered, and nothing counted. It was a truce to all things. No rules, no self-awareness, no battles, no nothing. Pure excitement, hopes, and dreams. And then the greatly anticipated due day came and went. Another day, and another. Then a huge sigh of relief when he wasn't born on Christmas. And another day, and yet another. Finally, ten days over his due date, my obstetrician decided we should induce before my son got too big. And in that moment, my birthing plan imploded.

After thirty-six hours of labor with no meds, I had only dilated five centimeters. They calculated that, at that rate, it would take me another thirty-six hours to dilate to ten centimetres, the minimum amount to deliver a baby naturally, and that by then, I would be too tired to push. C-section was declared the safest option for all. Good call, no doubt, but for the first time ever in my adult life, things were completely out of my control.

The irony was that the thing I thought I was controlling was actually a boat thrashing about on river rapids, headed towards a drop the size of Niagara Falls. Ultimately, if you are not sailing towards the realization of your Soul, you're most definitely directed towards a nosedive of some kind, or you'll simply repeat the same behaviours over and over.

I was utterly terrified and abruptly awake. I cried and let go of my false sense of control and completely surrendered. *"Let it be, let it be…whisper words of wisdom, let it be,"* played on my internal FM station.

My son was born at 18:03, a screaming vision of joy and radiance. My heart burst wide open with love and utter awe.

Then there was a sudden amount of commotion in the room. My surgeon told me I had a fibroid the size of a grapefruit and that he would need to remove it with the help of another surgeon. As Surgeon #2 entered, I began to bleed out, and one of the nurses fainted, landing on the floor with a loud thud. There were whispers and comments I couldn't make out, and suddenly I felt myself slipping out of my body.

What? Now?

I was unexpectedly taken back to that Saturday morning when I was eight. Birth and death are just different faces of the same coin. Birth is the taking in of the Soul and death is the releasing of it.

I was immediately overtaken with an immense willpower to live, to stay and be witness to this incredible life force, my son. I dug my stubborn hooves in and told Death to beat it. Tears tickled my cheeks, and I refused to close my eyes. "No," I whispered. "Not today. Please." I made a quick and quiet pact with Death: I would devote myself to being the best mom I could be and I would always put my son first. Always. I began to sing a Beatles song as a way to stay present in my body. "Ain't got nothing but love girl eight days a week…"

Then, suddenly I began to feel the operation. This was strange and traumatic, but it served a purpose; it brought me back into my body in an instant. Death left the room and there was a furious scramble to stop the bleeding and pump up the pain meds. Before I could really care, I was all sewed up and breastfeeding my newborn miracle.

Death is a powerful force in the journey of awakening. Even

though I didn't die that day, I felt its presence just enough for it to light a real fire under my unconscious derriere.

And so, on the day of his arrival, this remarkable being who cast me as his mother in the movie of his *Life* awakened me to my very first lesson: Let go, you don't have control. You never did, you never will. It's all an illusion wrapped in your disjointed Ego. A spiraling rhumba of smoke and mirrors. Be the director of your Soul, not your Ego.

Parenthood

Parenthood is, of course, a challenge on every level. You never really kill the disconnected Ego, but when you first give birth, it gets put in the basement in a chest with all the old toys. The lid is closed, and the Ego is told to be quiet or it might wake the baby. This was my experience in the first weeks of becoming a mother.

From my perspective, it appeared that my husband's disconnected Ego was really struggling with the new demands and lack of sleep. I was unable to validate him, or feed his emotional needs, and neither was our newborn. Instead, we both demanded things of him; his time, his help, and his emotional support.

I was suffering from undiagnosed baby blues and having difficulties breastfeeding. I had a tube attached to my nipple that fed my son extra milk because I was not producing enough. This method allowed him to get what he needed while his sucking stimulated my supply. I was determined for him to get all the nutrients that can't be found in any formula for at least six months. But my husband had to hold the tube above my head to let gravity do its part. At this point, our son was feeding every four hours and it was a two-person job every time. Exhaustion slammed us like a tropical storm.

At three weeks postpartum, my husband decided to go to LA to supervise the colour correction of a project he had done in the autumn. I begged him to stay, literally down on my hands and knees in a slobbering pool of drool and tears. I was so terrified to be left alone with my baby, the complicated breastfeeding ritual, and the blues.

He seemed not to feel that the situation was as dire as I portrayed, nor that it warranted his participation. He insisted that millions of women had done this before me, so why was I deficient? At that point, sunlight dipped below the horizon of my heart, and I felt the rise of my survival kit floating to the surface of my awareness.

I followed him with my gaze as he got into a taxi to the airport. He looked up at me in the window and smiled. His look of delight was far too brimming for my liking—it read: *R E L I E F.* In that moment, I understood and learned a most valuable lesson: *How long a person chooses to love or support you emotionally will never be your decision.*

The first year of being a new parent is exhausting, as a couple or alone. I was trying to be the best mom I could be, which for me meant putting my career on hold. What was completely unexpected was how my son's connectedness tugged at my spiritual cords of consciousness. His pure embodiment of love surged over me again and again like a tidal wave and began to erode my confused and misguided Ego, little by little. *You must blaze on. You are much more than you know.*

In a moment of clarity in the early hours one spring morning while breastfeeding my son, I experienced an overwhelming sense of oneness. Oneness with my son, but also with something bigger than us, the oneness of being. Of peace. Of surrender. I wept a waterfall, understanding that nothing beyond that connected state of blissful being was of any importance. Connection. Co-creation. Love. That was all there was. All that was important. The only thing that truly mattered. I laughed more tears at the sheer simplicity of it all. The Beatles were right.

My son's continuous barrage of love washed away my tired and swept my darkness downriver like mud during a monsoon. In my exhaustion, I had no stamina left to fight. I was stripped of all pretense and agenda, of every response to play the Ego game. I was sustaining my son's every need and could only exist in a state of love, acceptance, or giving. That was all. My fast-growing football-sized bundle of joy was teaching me that feuding or controlling was meaningless, that I was stronger and brighter than my shadow self.

The Shadow

Carl Jung, psychologist, psychiatrist, and founder of analytic psychology refers to the shadow as an unconscious aspect of the personality that the conscious ego does not identify in itself, or the entirety of the unconscious, i.e., everything of which a person is not fully conscious.

I began to see that, for the better part of my life, I had either tried to outrun my shadow, or let it take the lead. I recognised now that I would have to accept and integrate it for the polarity that it was. Just as the moon brings light in the nighttime, so the shadow brings darkness to the day. Both are equal and important parts of the whole. I found myself considering the powerful space between these polarities. *Is that where I might find peace?*

Our financial situation was beyond repair at this point, and my husband was not getting any work in Canada. We toyed with the idea of me staying in Canada with pup and tot, and him travelling back and forth to visit, but financially it wasn't feasible. We had no other alternative than to move the entire clan back to Santiago. We couldn't afford our own place, so we moved in with my mother-in-law and her two cats. Abuela (Grandma in Spanish) was very generous to accommodate this "intrusion," and she did it with grace and an open heart.

My husband was able to work and generate some income, and I took care of baby with a very hands-on grandma nearby. Moxie herded invisible sheep in the yard and yapped and snarled at the neighbouring Great Dane. I spent most of my time in a room off-limits to cats, or outside to avoid the histamine assault. I pushed my baby in a stroller around the perimeter of the house, creating dizzying circles as a way to get exercise and get my bundle of love to sleep.

It was an isolated existence, as we were in a tiny village south of Santiago without a car. And there it was once again, that strange sort of self-imposed confinement. This time for six months.

At the end of those six months, I really longed for freedom. From my allergies, mostly, but also freedom from isolation and pollution. With our finances looking up, we finally decided that it would be best if our son and I moved back to Canada.

We returned in delightful July, and liberation never tasted sweeter. There were mommy-and-me programmes, no cats in sight, and an activity-filled park nearby, with climbers and a wading pool, which we delighted in every day. My son had cousins to play with, and we began to create an incredibly diverse and fun routine.

My husband travelled back and forth and, although it wasn't ideal, we really hoped it wouldn't last forever. Work options in Canada began to roll in, and then, one month later, quite out of the blue, my husband was offered a movie abroad. I'd finally received some relief with our newfound routine, and I couldn't fathom the idea of being uprooted again. I told him I wouldn't go.

A few weeks later, another film was offered to him. This

time, he declared that this flick was the opportunity of a lifetime (aren't they all?). He accepted it in a New York minute before bouncing it off me. That sudden coup was like a hard yank on an old-fashioned French toilet. My stability and newfound balance were flushed into the sewer. With no delay, he departed for Barcelona to meet his true partner—his career. A good marriage is like finding the ultimate teammate, and yet, for the most part, I felt like a lonely loon on a lake. It was obvious that we were not great allies in parenthood and were both very much married to different things, he to his career and me to motherhood. My son and I were meant to join him in his perfect Heaven a few weeks later. And so, a new trend began— film trumped family.

Our son's first word was *ball*, which seems fitting, considering his endless love and passion for the sport of football (soccer). His second word was *aerpwane*. He pointed to the sky every time he saw an airplane and said, "Daddy *aerpwane*." At his tender young age, he understood that Daddy was coming and going by means of the sky rather frequently.

We'd already moved twice in my son's first six months of life, and I just wanted to settle down in the worst possible way. My husband had been quite protected from the sleepless nights, as he slept in another room while we lived in Santiago. For all intents and purposes, his life hadn't changed, except now he had the most adorable son to love and play with. Having been brought up in countries like Canada and Sweden, where men are very hands-on and involved in child-rearing, I was at a loss for how to bring my husband's expectations and understanding into the modern age.

Barcelona proved to be more of the same. His shooting schedule was a nightmare, and there were days when he slept while we were awake and vice versa. The single, childless film crew lived upstairs from us in the building where we were staying and partied every Friday and Saturday night until the wee hours of the morning. When I asked my husband to have them turn it down so we could sleep, he refused on the grounds that it *wasn't cool*. Once again, his reputation and standing took the lead.

I tried to make the best of a less than ideal situation and explored the architecturally rich and vibrant city alone with my nine-month-old. I quietly counted the days until we would be back to regular programming in Canada. I made a secret pact with myself—never again.

About a year later, once we were back in Vancouver, happily settled into a new pattern of playtime and naps, I discovered my husband was having an affair. It rattled my world like an earthquake, and my house of cards collapsed. Nausea set in first. Then doubt. *Is this really happening?* Nah, there must be some mistake. But the evidence was staring me in the face, and I couldn't ignore it. My spirit shattered like broken glass, and my body filled with sadness and disappointment. A ferocious tsunami of dejection rose within me and changed the very colour of my hair. Then the rage whirled through my soul and steeped my entire being in a desert mirage. Infidelity is a hard pill to swallow no matter what the circumstances. The notion of contrast was blasting notes of anguish and ecstasy into my reality once again. *I had known anguish like this before, but would I ever know the flip side? Would I ever know ecstasy?*

I recognised once again that a person's behaviour tends to have more to do with their own internal struggle than anything to do with them loving, or not loving, someone else. And with that premise smashed into my awareness with such brute force, grace whispered sweet songs of forgiveness in my ear. I began to understand why seeking validation or adoration from an external source can only ever lead to suffering. The only person who will never stop loving you, ever, is you, your inner being, your innate, instinctual Soul-self.

Needless to say, we divorced soon thereafter—*No way to*

delay that trouble comin' every day, as Zappa sang. I was inwardly disappointed that he made not the least attempt to try and win me back. Nothing. No apologies. No begging. No Romeo and Juliet balcony moment. Nada. He never explained himself or tried to salvage the marriage. He simply slithered away like a cowardly snake and said yes to divorce and handed me full custody. I would come to understand that his betrayal and behaviour were a blessing, and that ultimately it would lead me to the freedom I so desperately yearned for.

As much as I wish I could say I acted with compassion during this time, it's just not the truth. There was nothing even remotely poetic about me. I felt very much alone with this new notion of I-choose-to-be-with-her-not-with-you. The last rays of hope plunged into my ocean. I would have to start over.

Superpower

We all have our own superpower(s). A trait or traits that define us because of the hardships or triumphs we've experienced and make us who we are. I have two superpowers: sixth sense and resilience.

I was born with the first, an ability we all share upon arrival, but most of us lose this treasure as we plummet further and further into the senseless womb of the Ego and self-limiting beliefs.

The second, resilience, is something I developed over the years. I never realised how resilient I was until I had to forgive someone who wasn't sorry and raise a child on my own. As a woman and mother, I was swirling in a tornado of self-inflicted activity and expectation. I felt pressure to be all things to all people; the understanding and accommodating ex-wife, the accomplished and self-reliant daughter, the selfless and loving mother. I, like most women, was expected to be all these things every day while strolling in an air of ease with a smile on my face. It's unsustainable. Something, somewhere, is going to give.

Resilience, to me, is about the ability to bounce back, to rebuild, to be flexible and recognise what is offered in the present moment and accept it for what it is. It's about understanding that nothing lasts forever, and what is a problem today could very well be gone tomorrow. It's about asking for help or reaching out to a partner, friend, or family member when it's all too much. It's about practicing kindness to yourself when you're completely overwhelmed and finding strength when all seems lost. And, above all, it comes back to perception. Is this situation *tragic* or is it an opportunity to *grow* and *learn*?

I was back in therapy and coming to the understanding that the constant factor in my two broken relationships was me. Sure, my partners were broken in their own ways, but I was not trying to fix them, I was trying to find *my* wholeness. I realised that betrayal comes in many forms, and I took a good look at myself. *Had I possibly betrayed myself? Had I pressed the launch button into marriage before truly knowing who I was marrying and why I was marrying him? What secret bargain had I made with myself; was it conscious or unconscious?* Down I went into the labyrinth of my shadow self, looking for answers, looking for my truth.

I began to understand that in order to listen to the innate call from within, we must remember to be playful, to sing and dance, laugh and be in awe. Our children, and society at large, cannot afford to lose us to burnout, disease, or mental health issues. We must love and protect ourselves and rebound with resilience whenever we go astray.

It's difficult, as so many of us were raised by the Baby Boomer generation of women who were frequently told what to do, and how to behave, and stood on quicksand foundations of Self. If they spoke out against injustice, they were met with physical force and insults. But we do no one any service by strutting through life cloaked in "accommodating" and "pleasing." The longing to be authentic beckons us at every moment. It's our inner call to action, to alignment with self. It's an integral ingredient of our magic sauce.

Children teach us to be flexible, another component of resilience. We create routines to give them structure and comfort, and they tear them down at every turn by simply *being* and *listening* to their inner calling. That call might be to create art on the wall when you're trying to get them to day care, or to pour a bowl of cereal on their cousin's head just before your friend's wedding. It's an instinctual feeling, and they act on it without hesitation. It's their innate wild nature, and although it can be frustrating for parents at times, it's amusing and beautiful to watch. For me, resilience played a key role in my ability to find my way back to my instinctual, playful self.

At two and a half, my son and I got on with life, and his dad came to visit every eight to ten weeks. The dust finally settled, and we found a rhythm. I was able to get my bearings and went to therapy once a week to learn how I'd come to play this repeating tune over and over.

During one of my evening bath extravaganzas with my son, I was unexpectedly flooded with the awareness that my son was the same age I'd been when I was put up for adoption. I became cognizant of two things: how difficult it must have been for my mother to give me up, and the fact that I was experiencing single parenthood similar to the way my mother had. My son was always super silly and loved music. At that age, he liked to sit on the potty and strum the guitar. It was his thing. I wondered what my thing had been at that age, and suddenly I had a deep understanding of why giving me up had broken my mother's spirit. I squirted the squeaky water toys and reveled in the game of splashy-splashy with my son. I swore an oath to myself never to abandon him.

All that fun and joy brought me to the understanding of

how much my biological mother had loved me. For her to put me first, to give me away at the expense of her own happiness, was an indication of a profound motherly love. At least, that was how I decided to understand that part of my story.

A few years after I'd put my search for my biological father to rest, I awoke some time just before midnight to a tap on my shoulder. I was single and not sharing my bed with anyone, so I panicked and sat up erect, thinking there was an intruder in my house. What I saw was a man sitting at the end of my bed with his back to me. He was not of the flesh. My heart was racing. *Who was he? What did he want?* I reached for the phone, palms sweating, and called Martina. She was able to tap into the energy and devised that he was a benevolent energy and no threat. He'd come because I'd asked him to. *What?* I had no clue what she was on about. Martina suggested I ask him to leave if he made me uncomfortable, which I did. He vanished into thin air. I stayed up all night writing in my journal with the light on because I was too afraid of what other strangers might be drifting in the dark with me. The date was July 3, as marked in my journal, coincidentally the same date I had rescued Moxie from the streets of Santiago some years earlier. It would be many years before I finally learned the significance of this date.

From the Inside Out

The third shift was altogether energetic and completely unexpected—it was akin to something out of a science fiction novel. I was invited to Martina's house for dinner with a group of spiritually liked-minded people. Back then, I still felt somewhat out of place in groups of spiritually inclined people, but this flock of friendlies was super welcoming. There was a man there, another medium, who said he acted as a *conduit* for a dynamic energy from the Pleiades. He asserted it was "healing." In other words, it would make you notice your shadow so you could reconcile and integrate it. The concept of a healer, I believe, is simply a person who has the ability, and possibly the alignment and awareness, to guide you to those parts of yourself that are wounded and still need integration. But nobody heals anyone else, only *you* can heal *you*.

I didn't know much about energy at the time, but I tried to have an open mind. After dinner, we all sat down and did a group meditation led by this man. After about five minutes, I suddenly felt an energetic force gently press upon my entire body. I can only describe it as a continuous wind pushing against me. Not so forceful that it could knock me over, but enough that I couldn't quite resist. No one in the room had moved, and no one was touching me. This strange pressure pushed my head backwards and my mouth opened. I felt a torrent of energy stream into my body. After about a minute, the flow ceased, and the gentle gust released me. I tried to move my neck, but I felt like I'd been in a head-on collision. When I tried to stand up, the furniture and faces spun like a disco ball. Sitting was quite literally all I could do for the rest of the evening.

It was the most bizarre experience I have to report, to date. I felt the energy spread throughout my body—every cell was vibrating with a new frequency. Everything tingled. After the meditation, I told the man what had happened, and he answered matter-of-factly, "Yes, this has happened before. The energy I channel seems to choose certain individuals to activate." *What the heck did he mean exactly by* activate? *Activate what?* As the evening progressed, the buzzing throughout my entire body increased. It was as if I were suddenly plugged into a socket and electricity was running through me instead of blood.

Later that evening, following my first tasty vegan meal, the same man demonstrated his energy work on everyone. When it was my turn, he asked me to sit in a chair. He stood behind me and told me to close my eyes and relax. Immediately, I felt a transfer of heat into my back, and a bizarre swirling sensation around my head. I felt pure bliss and love wash over my entire frame. And then a strange stirring within me—something rising up and out of me. I can only describe it like a pebble being sucked up a tube. This pebble was a deeply rooted pain, an entombed trauma. It was abruptly released, and tears began to run down my face like freed ants. I understood that the emotions gushing forth were related to a feeling of being unloved and abandoned. With the man's encouraging words, I released all those negative emotions. I suddenly heard a woman's voice gently soothe me, *"Let go. You are loved—you are very, very loved."* I cried a river for all the years I'd ever felt neglected.

That evening introduced me to energy in a most profound way. I was pulsing with new voltage, and I quickly understood that by altering someone's energetic vibration you can alter their resonance, and therefore, their well-being.

The next morning, I woke with the same electric purring running through me—and it did not abate. The following night, I had a dream about two red snakes. The way they moved in an intertwining pattern reminded me of the staff of Hermes (caduceus) and I intuitively understood that this force was medicinal, or *healing* in some way. *What was happening to me?* In the months that followed, I was quite unexpectedly catapulted into a frenzy of reading and absorbing knowledge at an accelerated rate. I read books on quantum physics and entanglement, sacred geometry, the Mayans, Buddhism, Hinduism, cosmology, Native American tribes, and a mathematician named Bonaventura Cavalieri and his work on the emergence of the method of indivisibles. I took notes and continued to be interested in bizarre new subjects, even if I didn't completely understand them. My consciousness seemed to be evolving at an incredible rate. I was like Pac-Man on speed. Gobbling up unfamiliar subjects I'd previously had no interest in.

I began to understand that geometry is a language unto itself, patterns of consciousness that create physical things. Physics has always been an interest of mine, but my understanding of it is, shall we say, rudimentary. Quantum mechanics is notorious for tangling people's brains into a ball of confusion. Even the greatest minds of our day admit to not completely understanding the existing theories. I began to contemplate the idea that something observed collapses into matter, and unobserved it remains in its original state, a wave. Therefore, I conceptualized that our conscious point of attention might be able to change the state of something. Whatever we can imagine, we can make happen. A simple idea, yet complex at its core.

Interestingly enough, this led me back to Buddhism and the concept of interconnectedness and that prevailing feeling I had of oneness with my son and the Universe. Buddhism uses the word *interconnectivity* to describe how everything in the Universe is intimately interrelated. The idea that we are separate entities, distinct from the world around us, is considered to be an illusion. The true nature of humanity and reality is of a complete unification, or oneness. Now science defines quantum entanglement in a similar way: when two particles interact with each other, they become entangled, developing a special connected relationship with one another. Quantum entanglement seems to point to a true oneness with the Universe. At this time, I discovered a book at the library called *The Quantum and the Lotus*, written by Matthieu Ricard, a trained molecular biologist working in the lab of a Nobel Prize–winning scientist, and professor of astronomy Trinh Xuan Thuan. This book expanded my mind even more. Through the course of their dialogue, Matthieu and Thuan offer new understanding of the many ways in which science and Buddhism confirm and complement each other. Matthieu writes, "Knowledge of our spirits and knowledge of the world are mutually enlightening and empowering." I began to feel like I was seeing and understanding our world for the first time, and for its true nature, not the illusory one.

The principle of unity and the idea of oneness pervaded my every thought. I walked out into the world of my busy city and realised that my perception had changed. Instead of seeing the rat race scurrying before me, I saw the connectivity between all things. I was having my very own Luc Besson *Lucy* moment. I suddenly understood that I was a piece of the whole and the guy sitting across from me on the subway was an extension of me, and me to him. Everything is connected in a grand, intricate, harmonious, cooperative way.

In that instant, I truly understood hurting someone is only hurting yourself. I found myself talking to a homeless man on the street one day. I asked him where he was from, what his hopes and dreams were. I shared my lunch with him and enjoyed his company on the cold concrete sidewalk. Something profound was happening to me, and as much as I was scared out of my wits by the sheer ferocity of it all, I was simultaneously so glad to finally be able *to see*. My reservoir of compassion was increasing. I began to consider that this way of seeing was possibly the way Spirit must see. No boundaries or limitations, but interconnectedness on a grand scale, held together by only one thing. Love.

I was having my very own overview effect experience but without being an astronaut launched in space. The overview effect is a cognitive shift in awareness reported by some astronauts during space flight while observing Earth from space.

I'm not at all surprised; the view alone would be major cause for a shift in perspective.

I had little idea of what was happening to me and at times I got really scared that I was going off the deep end. When that happened, I would launch myself into my son's world, where I'd immediately become grounded in his love and activities.

I sought out meditation man and asked him for some explanation and help. *What the heck was happening to me?* He didn't have any answers, which was even more unsettling, however he did introduce me to the Bach Flower Essences, which helped to dial down the strange energetic symptoms I was having.

I was unexpectedly drawn to articles on the internet about starseeds and all things related to Arcturus and Sirius. I learned that a starseed is a Soul who first incarnated somewhere beyond this planet, and in many cases, has experienced life in other galactic systems or on other planets. I began to have visitations from inter-dimensional beings and felt a sudden deep connection to dolphins and whales.

Meditation became really easy for me at this point, and I actually preferred to be in a meditative state than in the illusory world of the matrix. It felt more benevolent and real to me. Dolphins began to appear in my meditations, playful and communicative. They introduced the idea of conversing via symbols and sound. I felt an urgency to meet these creatures in the wild and found the website of a woman who did dolphin seminars in Hawaii. I signed up right away. Three months later, I was swimming in the warm waters of Hawaii with pods of bottlenose.

And still, the information delirium continued; quantum physics, Buddhism, Zen Buddhism, the Tao, all sorts of artists, mathematicians, great thinkers, and inventors. I was like the boy in the children's story *The Incredible Book Eating Boy* by Oliver Jeffers, gobbling up books and knowledge as fast as the impulse hit me.

Just when I thought I was really going to blow a gasket, my son confirmed what I had suspected. At the innocent age of three, he said to me after an hour of splashy-splashy in the bathtub, "My guides sometimes go to 6398 school. So do you." He then jumped right into his pajamas and requested I read *The Snail and The Whale* for the hundredth time.

That comment helped me because my humanness wanted to quantify what was happening, and school and learning was something I understood. Whether the school was called "6398" or the course was titled "How the Universe Truly Works 101" didn't matter. I now felt like I understood what was happening to me; my conditioned programming and nervous system were rebooting, and in so doing, my perspective of myself and the world around me was shifting. Compassion was filling each of my chakras, and I had a deepening desire to live a life of integrity with my own Spirit. I was a student of the cosmos, expanding my awareness and broadening my perception.

At this point, certain foods and beverages just didn't sit well with me. I stopped eating red meat and pork. I dropped all things caffeinated and alcoholic. I began eating chlorophyll and spirulina. I switched to an aluminium-free deodorant and suddenly felt like I was a walking beacon. Certain friends began to simply not *feel* right. A handful of them fell away like chipped paint and fresh friends brushed my walls with new luminosity.

Breath

One day, rather unexpectedly, I found myself drawn to this book called *Nothing in This Book Is True, but It's Exactly How Things Are* by Bob Frissell. I had become a seeker, and this book contained many profound truths that deeply resounded with me (though not everything in this book resonated with me, just to be clear). One of them was the idea that breath was a gateway to the great unknown.

I became enthralled with the idea of harmonizing the body. That meant being mindful of what foods and liquids I put into it, the breathing techniques I used, the exercise I did, the content I watched, the books I read, the stories I listened to and told, the music I listened to, and the self-talk inside my head. I came to understand that everything affects us in a positive or negative way, absolutely everything. *Why?* Because we are vibrational energy and everything around us is, too. Wave frequencies travelling here and there interfering with our own resonance. Nothing rests, everything is in a constant state of motion and vibration. It became obvious to me that our Universe and everything in it is merely matter (originally light and sound possibly) and this *matter* is energy in a state of vibration.

I couldn't stomach watching the news any longer, and violent TV shows and movies were a thing of the past. I became suddenly overly sensitive to lies and violence. A lot of my world seemed to be out of resonance with the new *me*. It was as if everything was up for review, and if it wasn't in *attunement* with me, then it miraculously disappeared from my life.

These topics of resonance and breath lead me to yoga and Pilates. I began to do a regular restorative yoga class at my local YMCA and found the teacher to be *attuned* to my frequency. Pilates was not offered at my Y, so I found a small studio nearby and purchased what I could afford, two classes. My Pilates instructor insisted on teaching me pranayama breathing, diaphragmatic or deep-belly breathing. I enjoyed it immediately. I felt invigorated yet relaxed, and somehow more connected with my body as a whole. A few days later, while waiting in line at the grocery store, I grazed a fashion magazine and found an article about a model who believed sunbathing without SPF was actually good for your body. I didn't finish the article but instead raced home utterly consumed with an idea.

When I got home, I stashed the groceries in the fridge and went up to my bedroom. The sun flooded the room with an orangey glow. *Perfect.* I grabbed my yoga mat and purposefully lay down in the warm stream of sunrays. I began to perform pranayama breathing and counted the breaths in my head. As I reached fifteen, I noticed something shifting within me; then came sixteen; and at seventeen something quite unexpected happened. I was suddenly outside of my body. I hadn't consciously intended to do this but there I was, floating outside my body. My Soul had been released and was looking back at my physical body. I still had all my thoughts and decided to take another deep-belly breath. I was instantly out in the cosmos somewhere. I looked around, trying to locate something familiar and noticed our blue-and-white jewel, a speck in the far distance. *Whoa.*

An ethereal thread like an old-fashioned, curly telephone cord seemed to be attached to me, and I knew that my human body and Soul were connected via this etheric cord. I looked around, totally amazed. I whispered to myself, *Let's keep going.*

My Soul then shot off and I found myself travelling through a sea of white light. It was bright at first, and then became so blinding I couldn't see. My human body responded physically, and tears streamed down my face in reaction to the resplendence. It lasted for a long while. I sailed through the luminous brilliance and then suddenly found myself suspended in a world I can only describe as an endless ocean of saffron-orange and sunflower-yellow hues. I felt like I was swimming inside a Sunkist lava lamp. So peaceful in its essence. A sea swell of honeycomb yellow and calypso orange. Benevolent and healing. An ever-flowing coulis of peace and love.

Then, I heard voices. Many voices. This infinite abounding lake of light was one big ocean of energetic consciousness, and I could hear the chatter of millions of Souls. So many voices, so many languages, so many consciousnesses. An expansive core, teeming with activity, brimming with life. Like a bobbing buoy, I observed this incredible expanse, awestruck. A Boundless Core of Consciousness.

I was suddenly reminded of the heavenly vision I'd had following my miscarriage. The ethereal traveller had shown up in my vision surrounded by these same orangey-yellow rays. My brain then rationalized that this must be the place where we all come from before we incarnate, and where a part of our Soul resides while we're experiencing our physical incarnation. *The Boundless Core of All Consciousness. The Sea of Souls, possibly?* I questioned whether this was also the place we go back to when we die. *Was this the still point that T. S. Eliot spoke of in his poetry? Or perhaps the place of interval between lifetimes?*

I was quickly made aware that the energy of this place was revitalizing. A bath of rebirth. Of rejuvenation. A place of Soul cleansing and repair, as it were. In a flash, I understood that, during our lifetime, our Soul collected "debris" and that this Boundless Core reinvigorated the Soul, allowing it to renew. I could feel how my Soul was being replenished. Rebirth without death.

My heavenly rapture was abruptly concluded by the rational thought that I had to go pick up my son from day care. It was time to go. I soaked up every ounce of overflowing love, resurgence, and euphoria from that limitless *jus* of energy and light, and in just a thought and one deep breath, I was back in my physical body.

My perception of myself changed, and life as I knew it was never quite the same. I continued to have *Aha!* moment after *Aha!* moment for approximately ten months. At one point, I was quite concerned that the intensity of this experience would never slow down and that I would somehow erupt into a million splinters of light. I asked Martina for help, and she put me in touch with a woman in Arizona who quite quickly informed me that I'd had something called a "kundalini awakening." *Ah, OK, what is that?* I did a lot of research and discovered that this kundalini thingy did in fact correlate with my personal experiences. I discussed it with my yoga teacher, and he, too, confirmed it. I felt rather silly; I was seemingly the only person who had no idea what it was, and yet it was happening to me. Another fellow I met some time later called it a starseed awakening. I decided that the operative word was *awakening,* and whether it was preceded by another word or not didn't much concern me. I assumed that my experience of it, and with it, was unique to me anyway, so why bother with a label?

After a while, I began looking for a guru. I went to various Buddha and Zen centres. Ironically, they were always closed for a holiday, lunch, or some other siesta-like situation when I showed up. Not once, not twice, but seven separate times. I finally asked in meditation why this was happening. My inner voice stated matter-of-factly, "No one can teach you what you need to know. You are your own teacher." *Bugger me. Now what?* The enthusiastic and slightly hysterical nature of it all did finally taper off, and my frenzied conduct finally slowed to a horse's trot. It became quite manageable—I felt almost normal again.

This weird and wonderful energetic surge had propelled me into an intense investigation of greater meaning and understanding of how we, our world, our Universe, and the galaxy at large truly operate. I began to invest deeply in myself.

Forgiveness

My enraptured bath in the Boundless Core of All Consciousness led my awareness to two words: *oneness* and *forgiveness.* It took place approximately one year after my ex-husband left me for someone I thought of as a self-serving homewrecker. Up until that point, I'd been quite consumed by anger and resentment towards him and was having a difficult time managing these emotions. After the meditation with Martina's friend and my purifying dip in the Boundless Core, my awareness and consciousness shifted dramatically. One day, I simply stopped myself in all my bitterness and outrage and said out loud, *"Who am I to decide whom he should or shouldn't love?"*

From that moment forward, I kept close tabs on my reactive emotions and began a conscious effort to respond in full awareness and not react in unconscious agitation.

I made every effort to keep my ex in my son's life. I hosted him when he visited and insisted on us being together on Christmas and our son's birthday. My family gladly moved Christmas to the 26th one year to accommodate his schedule. I facilitated my ex in every conceivable way to allow the two of them to have the best relationship possible within this unfavourable, we-are-now-divorced-and-live-in-different-countries predicament.

I rose above my disconnected egocentric consciousness that wanted to punish him for being unfaithful and abandoning us. I outshined my seductive Ego that wanted to shame him for leaving me alone to raise our child. I was suddenly towering above my negative emotions, and instead of trying to drill sense or compassion into my ex's heart, I had a deep knowing that forgiveness was the only way forward—the only path that would benefit all three of us. The French have a saying, *"Tout comprendre c'est tout pardonner,"* which roughly translates to, "To understand all is to forgive all." That profound insight took me completely by surprise and set me on a new course.

This understanding startled me, and I was being asked to see life as it truly was, not as I wanted it to be. With this fresh perspective, I began to set a new tone and pace for our future. From that moment forward, I asked one simple question when making decisions pertaining to family: *Will this benefit my son?* Life got a whole lot easier after that.

When it comes to forgiveness, we can start by truly understanding that we are not responsible for anyone's actions.

We always have the choice to be reactive, or to respond and forgive. Many years ago, I chose to forgive my ex for his selfish conduct, and it redirected the course of my life in a positive way. When we align with the tone of forgiveness, it always leads to good things. Whenever I am tempted to stand in a place of judgement or reactivity, I use these quick affirmations to shift my thinking:

1. I choose not to judge his/her choices.
2. I choose not to be reactive.
3. I choose to forgive.
4. I choose to stay in my own lane of love and awareness.
5. To understand all is to forgive all.

Forgiveness is letting go of your reactive stance. It's all about redirecting your point of perspective and releasing any resistance you hold against a person or event until there is no energetic attachment. It quite immediately shifts your negative emotions to positive.

Forgiveness allows you to rise above the ash of anger and resentment, and ignites your higher perspective, immediately dissolving another person's ability to have power over you. It fills your spirit with unconditional love and releases the shackles of attachment. Nelson Mandela was imprisoned for twenty-seven years on Robben Island and experienced humiliation and solitary confinement on many occasions. When he became the president in 1994, he did not seek revenge on his former jailers; instead, he invited one of them to his inauguration. He rose above bitterness and rancor, and the rest, as we know, is history. I use his example with great humility to highlight my point. All roads of forgiveness lead to love.

Conscious Point of Attraction

As I began to make peace with my ex and my reactive self, I made a conscious decision to stay in my own lane. There was no point in getting all worked up over another person's actions or decisions, no matter how inappropriate I thought they were. His choice. His path. *And honestly, who was I to judge him?* I realised that people act according to the arrangements they have with themselves, with their own minds, and there's not one darn thing we can do about it.

However, I am human, and the momentum of this resentment had been building for some time, and in response, the cells of my body had created a magnificent kidney stone. Hard and unrelenting, just like my emotions and thoughts had been. The cells of your body are listening, so be conscious of your thoughts.

I awoke at 1:00 a.m. in excruciating pain and had to make a decision as to what to do. My two-year-old son was deep in the Land of Nod, and if I went to the hospital, I would have to wake him and bring him with me. Of course, I could call my parents and ask them to stay with him, that was the obvious choice, but instead I listened to an inner voice that said, *"Change your conscious point of attention and all will be well."*

I honestly had no idea how to do that. The pain was agonizing. I crawled over to my desk, dragging a blanket with me like lovable Linus from *Peanuts*. I sat in front of my laptop and began scrolling for a place to shift my attention. I googled comedy and came across Eddie Izzard. If you don't know who he is, look him up on YouTube. He's an openly straight transvestite who does stand-up comedy and is absolutely hilarious. Any one of his acts will have you in stitches. I began to watch his special *Dress to Kill* and was laughing myself to wellness in minutes. His impression of Christopher Walken doing Shakespeare and his infamous "Death Star Canteen" sketch had my point of conscious attention shifted instantly.

My crying was no longer due to pain, but from laughter. Laughter raises your vibrational resonance and brings you up and out of the critical bog. I simply chose to shift my perspective and not suffer through the pain. I giggled and cried until 7:00 a.m., at which point my mini-me awoke, ready for some fun-filled hours at day care.

The doctor I saw later that day immediately concurred that I had passed a kidney stone or two and prescribed Percocet for the pain. He was taken aback when I said I didn't need any pain meds. I explained how I had shifted my point of focus from suffering to laughter thanks to Eddie Izzard. Quite bewildered, he insisted he'd never known anyone to laugh through the passing of kidney stones.

After that, I chose to look forward and leave my ex and all his decisions behind. They were his, after all, and he would have to own them one day, not me. I also instantly understood that we can only respond to things from our individual conscious, or unconscious, place of understanding and awareness. At some point in time, not so long ago, I, too, had been behaving from an unconscious place of non-resonance. By judging him, I was, in fact, only judging myself—I let my scrutiny go.

We all have blind spots that tend to go unnoticed for the most part, because as the saying goes, "What you don't know won't hurt you." That statement is utter rubbish. Every experience you have in life is stored in the vast memory of your cells and quantum DNA. What you don't deal with will manifest in your body in some form, at some point in your life. The fact that I got kidney stones some months after I found out my husband was cheating on me was no coincidence.

We all live in our own situational comedy or tragedy, one where the greatest irony is that we've forgotten who we truly are. We're conditioned to believe we are powerless and that our biological evolution was purely accidental. Our bodies function every minute without our direction. The first cells that created this human body divided without any instruction from our minds, which didn't even exist yet. That first division went on to create a mind-blowing physical body. Our hearts beat, our blood flows, and our cells regenerate and attack unwanted bacteria without our minds telling them to do so. It's an astounding energy system that works exceptionally well, except for when our negative thoughts and non-resonant emotions get in the way. In the words of Kierkegaard, "Our life always expresses the results of our dominant thoughts." And a belief is simply a recurring thought. Science is now embracing research that will hopefully show that we humans have the ability to self-regulate on a multitude of levels.

Empath Qualities

With my newfound sensibilities, I had become more attuned to my own body, feelings, and thoughts (positive and negative), as well as those around me. I acquired the not-so-desirable aptitude for feeling other people's ailments. It was scary at first because I thought they were mine, but I quickly understood that if I left the proximity of the person who was ill, I soon felt well again. Of course, this also encouraged my self-imposed isolation, which was becoming my new normal.

One Sunday evening, at my parents' house for the customary weekly family gathering, an odd sensation took me over. We were all sitting around the table, debating and doing what families do, when suddenly I became completely unwell. I looked around to see whom I was picking up on and realised that no one at the table was under the weather. The usual antics and chatter prevailed. My mom commented on how I'd suddenly paled. I raced to the washroom just in time for my insides to turn on like a faucet. I was hunched over and immediately aware that *this was what death felt like. Am I dying?* After about ten minutes, the symptoms eased up, and I went back to my fine-feathered frisky self. I returned to the table and chalked it up to something I ate at lunch.

About thirty minutes later, we were alerted when the flashing lights of an ambulance pulled up two doors down. My dad went over to see if everything was OK and returned a little later on and delivered the sad news; a neighbour had died earlier that evening. Every hair on my body stood to attention and saluted me with instant recognition.

As things progressed, I also became aware of my *attunedness* with my son. I think a lot of parents have this awareness, an ability to know when your kid is hurt, feeling sad, or in possible danger. The emotion of whatever they're feeling runs through you so strongly, you can't ignore it. This is not unique to me by any means. However, one of the many incidents I experienced took me by surprise.

It took place when my son was about seven years old. I was driving home when suddenly I saw a flash of an image in my mind's eye of my son hitting his head really hard. The impact was forceful, and I felt a jerk in my body, followed by nausea. I knew it was real and not one of those dreamlike visions I sometimes get. I turned a corner and rerouted myself back to his school. When I arrived, the receptionist announced they were trying to reach me. My son had fallen on the ice and hit his head. He had a Kinder Egg–sized lump and a bad concussion. He had to sit out of all sports activities for two weeks, and I monitored him closely during that time period. Thankfully, he fully recovered and was back to the usual shenanigans in no time.

These types of experiences reassured me that my instincts and intuition were on point. It was also a lesson in confidence and in trusting myself and that mysterious ethereal cord linked between parent and child. Intuition is not much valued in our culture today. We've been taught to neglect and fear it. To me, it's by far one of the most important and useful tools I have in my handy kit of qualities. It's one that I cultivate and appreciate enormously.

The energetic purring within me had finally slowed down to a rhythmic pulse akin to a heartbeat. As my 6398 Intense Overview Awakening came to an end, I found myself wondering what else had been eluding me all these years. I was eager to participate in something meaningful, and even if I didn't know what that was yet, I assumed that for the time being it was raising my son. I continued to connect with my Soul-self and allowed compassion and my inner GPS to guide me. I continued to heal the disowned parts of myself, and I practiced the art of surrender, forgiveness, and deep listening. The fog of amnesia was finally lifting.

PART II

LIT FROM WITHIN

CHAPTER FOUR

2008-2011

"... once you learn how to die, you learn how to live."

—Mitch Albom, *Tuesdays with Morrie*

Up until this point in my life, I had been somewhat sheltered from death. My grandpa died when I was eleven and living a modest misery in Luxembourg, and our dog, who didn't like anyone but Dad, died when I was eighteen and away working for the summer, picking strawberries in the fields of southern Sweden. Apart from those two departures, death had always felt remote, something that happened to other people. I had yet to have the pleasure of meeting death as a teacher.

The day I met Jacob for the first time, he'd already left the bookstore he'd gone to almost daily since retiring—but had suddenly felt compelled to go back. He later described the sensation as being like the pull of a magnet because he had read all the newspapers and had no reason to return. He walked through the aisles of books aimlessly, pondering his purpose.

Then he saw a pair of rubber boots. Black with white polka dots, and he knew he had to speak to whomever was in them. He apparently had met a few women in his lifetime who had worn curiously delightful rain boots, and it seemed to be a sign, of sorts. He approached me cautiously and in a gentle voice asked, "Is that any good?"

I turned the book over in my hand—*The Okinawa Program.* I blushed slightly and replied, "No clue. I'm curious about seaweed." After an hour of remarkably effortless chitchat, I suddenly felt my blood sugar level drop and invited my new friend for a coffee. We sat for an hour jabbering away, and the seed of what would become one of my greatest friendships was planted.

As we got to know one another, I noticed his dainty hands fondling the side of the stiff paper cup. They hadn't seen a day of labor. I inwardly questioned why and got my answer a few moments later. Jacob was a hemophiliac. His blood didn't clot properly, so if he got injured, he was likely to bleed much longer than the average person. Therefore, his parents had kept him away from axe-throwing and the like, and encouraged non-life-threatening activities, such as reading, debating, and chess.

I found myself thinking how his hands might be more appropriately attached to a female body. His slender fingers stirred up fond memories of my old boyfriend in Sweden, Mr. True Love—he, too, had delicate, feminine hands. My mind skipped out of the café and over to Gothenburg for a jog down memory lane. It became obvious during the years that followed that my new friend Jacob reminded me a lot of Mr. True Love and the possibility of a return to Sweden began to seep into my awareness.

Jacob was a vibrant spirit and curious about everyone and everything. He wanted to know who I was, what I wanted, what made me tick, what made me happy or sad, how I managed as a single mom, what my dreams were—his curiosity exploded like popcorn in hot oil. He was the most genuinely inquisitive person I'd ever met. I quickly learned that Jacob loved his partner, Vivian, with all his heart and, although it was risky, he had agreed to undergo an aggressive new treatment for the hepatitis he had contracted through a blood transfusion. This was apparently doing his liver no favours. He spoke very briefly about this and quickly changed the subject back to me and my pursuit of Soul fulfillment. He disliked being defined by his illness and preferred to launch himself into conversation about any other topic.

Over the following months of 2008, I shared my wild and weird spiritual journey with him, of which he had no judgments, just more curiosity. Jacob had this magic ability to truly listen. He would hear your words and the subtler subtext of their meaning and then translate it into viable options for you. As I began to reveal my hopes and dreams to Jacob, it became obvious to us both that I had a great desire to write.

I had so many stories I wanted to share. One was the search for my biological mom and dad. With the tenacity of a woodpecker, I search for over eleven years for my biological truth, and Jacob said he would be very interested in reading that story—why had I not written it? I rambled on about my lack of this and inadequacy of that and how writing was for intellects and academics. Then I just stopped all the negative momentum and was brutally honest: *"I lack confidence."*

Jacob waved his hand like a magic wand and, with his infectious humour, said I'd have more than enough and that it was something I could build. He made a suggestion that changed the course of my life: if writing an entire novel was too intimidating, why not write my story in episodes, like a column for a newspaper? Such a simple suggestion, but it lit me up, and later that week I began writing my columns just for Jacob.

When one column of my story was complete, I printed it out and sent it to Jacob. He was my only reader and I eagerly awaited his comments. This went on for months and was the beginning of my journey as a writer and storyteller.

Hello from the Other Side

One sunny afternoon, after I'd sent eight columns to Jacob, I was in the bank depositing some cash. I hadn't noticed the music playing in the background until suddenly my awareness took me to the lyrics of the song. It was a Styx song:

> *"…I'm leavin', I must be on my way*
> *The time is drawing near*
> *My train is going…"*

I suddenly knew this was a message from Jacob and I burst into tears surrounded by bank tellers and forest green sofas.

I was overwhelmed with the knowing that Jacob was going to die and sincerely humbled at how the Universe is able to communicate with us if we listen and pay attention. Two days later, I received a somber telephone message from Jacob. He was in hospital—his liver was in decline. He needed a liver transplant.

I went to visit him in hospital and met his partner, for the first time. She was bubbly and vivacious, all things considered, and immediately made me feel welcome. Jacob was slightly jaundiced from his failing liver, and the prognosis was dire.

I handed him a smile and a bottle of "holy" water. I told him I'd talked good vibes into it. He said he would drink every drop. He laughed in his non-judgmental, supportive way and joked about how *holy* water could be my next booming enterprise. We all laughed as Jacob drank from the *holy* bottle.

I left that day completely numb inside. I went to day care and picked up my beautiful bouncy boy and was immediately launched into a world of laughter and hugs. It was a gloriously sunny day, so we went to the park to do my son's favourite thing—play football. We ran up and down, tackling each other, and my son decked me out over and over, scoring goal after goal.

I was acutely aware of the contrasting energies of the day: one so vibrant and full of life, and the other in decline and letting go. There were those polarities again, front/back, life/death.

Our tummies declared it was time for dinner, and we headed home. A man wearing headphones whizzed past us on his bike. He was singing really loudly, and all I heard was, *"Stayin' alive."* I cocked my head like an inquisitive owl and watched the man ride past. His voice soared out again, *"Stayin' alive!"* and then he disappeared down the tree-lined path. I smiled to myself because I intuitively understood this to be yet another message from Jacob. I inwardly told the Universe that I would respect Jacob's decision to stay or to go—not without a tear or two, though.

The next day around lunch, I went to the hospital. I called up to the room first to make sure it was a good time to visit and was told that Vivian would meet me at the coffee shop in the lobby. Vivian arrived about thirty minutes later with a noticeable spring in her step. She was so distinctly upbeat, I immediately knew something had shifted. She dragged me with haste to the elevators and told me that Jacob was having transplant surgery tomorrow! I smiled, recalling the cyclist from the day before.

Jacob's hospital room was filled with his immediate family. I remember feeling distinctly out of place, and yet on another level, I knew I was welcome. Introductions were made and, although Jacob was so frail, he was beaming from ear to ear. He said he was running low on *holy* water and could I bring more next time?

Through example, Jacob taught me that love, wisdom, and humour combined are the most powerful synergies in the world. He emphasized humour as a must-have.

After that, no news meant good news. I found out about ten days later that the surgery had gone off without a hitch, and that Jacob was recovering well and would be going home soon.

A few weeks later, I spoke with him on the phone. He was delighted to tell me he was no longer *Jacob* but *Normal*. With his new transplanted liver, he was no longer a hemophiliac! For the first time in his life, he had a liver that made normal blood-clotting factors. He was ecstatic about being alive.

In true *Normal* fashion, he focused all his attention on me and joked about how my rebirth had been tremendous, too. The more we discussed what he meant, the more I realised that he was a mirror for me. I might not have undergone an organ transplant, but my mind, body, and heart were undergoing major transformations.

We discussed how important it was to cherish every moment, and he suggested I make note of the most important things in my life and ask myself what needed to be changed. If there was something, then I should change it now, while I had my health.

While driving home that afternoon, I saw a large looming billboard that had a white, blank canvas on it. No commercial message had been placed there yet. Then I heard a whispering voice: *Who and what do you want on your canvas?* We all have a relatively new slate every morning when we wake up, a somewhat neutral vibrational resonance. We therefore have the opportunity to create positively with our thoughts, beliefs, and intentions. We quickly fill in our morning canvas with ideas and desires. It's important to be consciously mindful of what we add to our slate in the morning and throughout the day. It will gather momentum as we fill it in with the energy of our ruminations and fascinations.

Harmonizing

In what seemed like a random sequence of events, I was introduced to an architect named Jean Luca. Jean Luca was looking for a filmmaker to shoot a project he was working on with Dr. Ibrahim Karim, who had invented the science of harmonizing energy, which he called BioGeometry. He defined BioGeometry as "the science of establishing harmony between biological fields and their environment, through the use of a design language of form, colour, motion, and sound." BioGeometry combines Pythagorean harmonics, the history of architecture, Ancient Egyptian temple science, and German and French Physical Radiesthesia to form a modern "Physics of Quality." Dr. Karim built upon this foundation and found the energies that contribute to health in biological beings.

He discovered ways to create these energies and studied their beneficial effects on diseases such as hepatitis C, reversing electromagnetic field sensitivity, growing plants without pesticides, and raising chickens without use of antibiotics.

As human beings, we are all receptors of resonance, and see electromagnetic radiation in the range of 400 to 700 nanometers and call it "colour." We hear compression of airwaves and call it "sound." Dr. Karim discovered that higher harmonic resonance was beneficial to the health of humans, animals, and plants.

Together with a producer friend, we came up with a film proposal and budget. Although we never made the film about their work, a new friendship was born, and I personally began to apply BioGeometry to everything in my life. There was a particular spot in my house that I knew was "off" because every time I put a plant there, regardless of what kind of plant it was, after a few weeks, it would inevitably grow brown spots and begin to wilt and die. Jean Luca harmonized my house and yard using BioGeometry. Although it was difficult to quantify exactly what had changed, I felt the difference, and my plants no longer died when placed in that particular location.

Not all vibrations are created equal, and science can now verify by measurement that most things carry different vibrational frequencies. We live in a world where we consume more information on a daily basis than ever before. If you believe, as I do, that all things are made of energetic vibration, then I'm sure you probably feel compelled to be responsible and somewhat finicky about what you ingest in all areas of your life.

The Talking Madonna

I visited Jean Luca one day at his forty-nine-story apartment. As you can imagine, the view of the city sprawl was spectacular. We sat and talked for a long while, and then he went to the kitchen to get us some water. I was peacefully minding my own business when suddenly I heard a voice that was not Jean Luca's. I looked around for a person and saw no one. I stood up and walked towards a cabinet full of glistening glasses. I felt a fool, but I swore the voice was coming from the cabinet. Then the voice spoke again. *"For those who can hear me, there is healing, love, and wisdom here."* Right there, in between the two cabinets, hung the most majestic painting of a Black Madonna. I looked around, a little befuddled. *Talking paintings?* It was an unusual take on talking heads. But tolerance and flexibility had taught me to be open and to embrace everything and everyone. *Why was this any different?* I stood there exchanging thoughts with this painted woman. It became clear that the resonance of the painting had been infused with a vibrational message by the consciousness of the *painter.* It had been permeated or *tuned* with the painter's thoughts and message. All the microscopic hairs on my body leaned towards the painting like metal shavings to a magnet.

Jean Luca returned and was delighted to see me admiring his Madonna. I looked at him and said, "Do you know that your painting speaks?" Jean Luca's expression lit up like fireworks on New Year's Eve. He informed me that this painting had been passed on in his family from one generation to another for centuries. He said his elders had spoken of the mysterious talking Madonna, but no one had heard her message for many a century. He beamed at me. "You are the first in many hundreds of years." I stood there in front of this incredible museum-worthy piece of magnificence and noticed how the colours began to shift and change. The blues became yellow and the reds became green. I felt almost as if I were hallucinating. The painting seemed to have consciousness, and as I tuned into this consciousness, it morphed and flowed. A confluence of energy was taking place between me and the painting. It was like kindred souls meeting, albeit from very different eras. There was a sense of union and mirroring. She was me and I was her. Her vibrational resonance matched mine, and so I was able to hear her.

This new awareness of being able to program things with vibrational messaging was a fascinating revelation. I found myself becoming more acutely aware of the consciousness of all things. Trees, flowers, rocks, water, animals, and so on. Little by little, I began to hear the delicate and delightful voices of many things.

Tuning

Jean Luca then introduced me to the work of a woman in Ithaca, NY, named Deena S. Deena graduated from Cornell University with a degree in Neurobiology and co-authored several papers showing the environmental damage caused by the use of pesticides. When she realised her own health was suffering from the effects of laboratory chemicals, she left the University and began studying violin making and acoustics. Jean Luca had completed her workshop on harmonic induction, or *tuning*, and was thrilled with his new skills and knowledge.

I immediately looked her up online and her website sent a positive purring throughout my body.

I reached out to her about her next workshop, but the timing never worked out with my ex's schedule. Kindly, Deena agreed to do a one-on-one weekend with me. Arrangements were made, and I drove south of the border in my little yellow-and-white Mini, eager to learn what *tuning* was all about.

I had no expectations and no clue as to the experience in which I was about to partake. The drive began with three hours on dull blacktop, with equally bleak scenery—and then, outside Ithaca, the stage setting completely changed. I was suddenly surrounded by lush green rolling hills and nibbling deer everywhere I looked.

I checked into my quaint B and B, "Morning Glory," and drove to Deena's house. Her property was a spectacular stretch of flourishing fields with a modern, Frank Lloyd Wright–inspired main building and one smaller house, where Deena and her dogs were waiting for me. Upon my arrival, a red-tailed hawk flew overhead. Deena said this was a great omen—we were in for a good weekend.

Deena's path to tuning had begun with violins. She and her husband at the time had a business together; he made the violins and she made fine adjustments to them. What she realised as she progressed in her work was that she didn't actually need to physically tune the instruments to change their resonance; she could do it with mental energy, with thought. She then discovered she could do it long-distance. Her musician clients and friends could hear the difference after Deena had *tuned* their instruments with her mind. Even to the musically untrained ear, the sound was noticeably different.

What this meant was that Deena was able to start *tuning* violins from a distance. Some of her clients would call her up before Philharmonic performances and ask her to mentally *tune* their instruments. Not a lot of questions were asked as to how she did this because the results were undeniable, and that was all that really mattered.

Deena is a no-BS kinda gal, and so, in true Deena fashion, we got right into it—no time like the now.

I naïvely thought I was somehow going to learn how to play the violin in a weekend and harmonize it, too. But that's not quite what happened. We started with breakfast utensils—a bowl and a metal spoon. Deena had me *play* the bowl with the spoon to get a sound. After doing that a few times, she asked me to close my eyes and go to that special place inside, similar to where you go when you meditate. Then she asked me to think of giving the sound a different *flavour* or resonance. I imagined the sound being fuller, like a pregnant belly. She then had me play the bowl again. The sound had changed! By observing the quality of the sound, I was able to change it.

She described what she heard to me: warmer and rounder. Whoa.

She smiled and insisted we keep going. After about an hour of influencing or *tuning* sound with mental energy, she said I could skip the workshop and jump straight to the advanced course. I'd apparently gotten the gist of tuning rather quickly and was ready for the next level—tuning instruments.

I drove back to my B and B that night in a blanket of black. It had been a very long day, and I'd used more mental energy in those few hours with Deena than I had in the last few months. I lay myself down and the soft quilt wrapped my body in profound sleep.

Over the course of that weekend, I learned that if it vibrates, it can be tuned mentally. And since absolutely everything in the Universe vibrates, absolutely everything can be tuned! Instruments, people, animals, traffic, food, and so on. The purpose of *tuning* is to help a person or situation find harmonious resonance and/or to alleviate discomfort.

Deena's book, *Ears of the Angels*, is a chronicle of her journey and transformation from acoustic researcher to healer—a must-read for anyone interested in harmonizing energies.

I returned home after my tuning extravaganza and couldn't help myself. I tuned everything. I was like a teenager with a new iPhone. Totally psyched and utterly obsessed.

First Tune

I was having lunch alone one day and ended up seated next to a sax player from Chicago. He was in town to play a gig, and we struck up a conversation. I asked him how his instrument was sounding these days. He looked at me with a slightly raised eyebrow and replied that it was fine except it was a bit pitchy on the high notes. He asked me if I played an instrument. I told him about Deena and my new-found hobby of tuning. He smiled and said, *"So, you a shaman?"* I replied that it was some kind of magic, and was he interested in his instrument sounding better? He laughed and said he would leave my name at the entrance of the club so I could come and perform my *magic* on his instrument before the show.

I arrived twenty minutes before he was to go on and was escorted backstage. I met the other band members and was promptly introduced to his sax. He joked that whatever I was going to do couldn't make it worse, so why the heck not give it a try? He played for me, and we both listened as he hit the high notes. The first word that came to mind was *scratchy*. He stopped and waited for me to perform a miracle. I tuned his sax, and he played it again. He was not at all impressed. Then I tuned him, and he played it. Again, not much had changed.

Time was running out, and the band was setting up onstage. He looked at me impatiently and said, "Hey, blondie, you tried. You're either crazy, or my sax is just stubborn. We cool." He patted me on the back and headed to the stage. I was completely befuddled and felt like a real sucker. But then I heard, "It's the reed." I jumped up and peered out onto the stage. Sax man looked at me like, *What now, crazy lady?* I ignored his justified look and asked, "Can you show me the reed?"

Like an even-tempered music teacher, he came over and pulled out the wooden reed from the mouthpiece and held it up for me to see. "Thank you." His patience was wearing thin, and he waved me off the stage.

I went backstage and tuned the reed for smooth silkiness in the high register. I then found a seat in the second row and relaxed into my red velvet chair as the band began to play. It was a cool jam, and the audience was digging the vibes. After a while, sax man started playing a solo, belting out a gazillion notes at a time. He then leaned back and made a sour lemon face and blew into the higher octaves. His eyes grew large as the sound soared out of his sax with a velvety resonance. He looked straight at me—eyes wide in amazement. He played the high register with ease, finished his solo, and the audience clapped enthusiastically. He held his instrument away from his body in astonishment while the band played on. He looked at me with a grin from here to Chicago, and pointed at me like I'd just scored a three-pointer to win the game. I smiled back, happy and slightly relieved.

At intermission, he came and sat at my table, full of excitement and questions. We chatted for a while, and then I stood up to leave. He gestured for my hand, and I held it out for what I thought was a traditional handshake, but he took it in both his hands and bowed over and kissed it. Even though I can't remember his name, I will always remember him fondly as my *first tune.*

The Hippies Were Right

It's all about vibration, man. Numbers are vibrational, just like everything else. After my third shift, I started seeing sequences of numbers everywhere, 11:11, 14:14, 16:16, 21:21, 777, 888, 222—on clocks, receipts, building numbers, license plates, my iPhone, my stove. I believe that my awareness shifted from the physical world of duality to the awareness of the nonphysical, and I began to tap into the Universal language of numbers, amongst other things. It seemed to also be a way for Spirit and my higher consciousness to communicate with me. I tend to be a person who wants to know how things work and what it all means. I always feel the need to qualify and quantify things, but I quickly learned that the only way to understand these numbers and their meaning (if there was one) was to let go of any preconceived idea of what they meant and simply feel for an understanding.

It came to me that seeing these numbers was simply an indication of my own vibrational stance and resonance. *But how so?* My mind needed to qualify it. It was described to me as being like another person in the room pointing to the numbers: "*Hey, look!*" and you look. That other person in the room is your Higher Self. So, my Higher Self was guiding me to look, because it knew those numbers were meaningful to me and they would make me understand that something poignant was going on. That poignant going-on was simply me letting go of the old paradigm and being in tune with the new frequency of my own spiritual connection. It was evidence of a grand mystical connection—the energy of the Universe yielding to me, and me to it.

I see these types of number combinations all day long now, and it just makes me smile because I know I'm in that sweet zone of resonance with my Higher Self. Even as I wrote this, 5:55pm showed up on my screen saver while I went to get a snack! And just the other day, I woke up at 2:22 in the morning. When I took the dog out for a walk, the first thing I saw when I hit the street was 777 on a license plate of a car parked right outside my door. I then walked to work and saw another license plate with the numbers 888. The less I try to control my surroundings and simply let go and allow my higher consciousness to guide me, the more I see these numbers. And to me, that means I'm in the sweet zone of flow with my bigger Self.

When the energy of my Soul, the energy of another Soul, or my inner being have a specific message for me, they generally use songs to communicate with me. Songs encompass an overall feeling or mood, as well as specific words. Therefore, songs can be a very effective way of communicating a precise message, just as I'd learned with Jacob.

When You Least Expect It

In the early days of summer, I received a call from my godmother, Joyce. She'd been cleaning out her garage and found some old letters and an invitation to a friend's funeral. She described the card to me. On the front was the name of her late friend, Mark Theo Stewart, and on the inside was the date of his passing, July 3, 2000. Opposite this was a picture of Mark posing with his German shepherd dog. I was silent for a relentless moment. Synapses were firing. Dots were connecting. July 3 was the same day that ghost of a man had sat at the end of my bed with his back to me. *Was this all coincidence?* My inner knowing was saying no. It was him. It was my biological father. I explained to Joyce what had happened a year ago on July 3 and more about the guided meditation I'd done with Martina. I suggested that her deceased friend was my biological father.

Joyce was upset and explained that she had asked Mark,

time and time again, if he was the father, and yet he'd denied it. She was bewildered as to why he had lied.

The next day, we met at Café Luna, and she gave me the card to keep. There he was, in colour, with his dog with the pointed ears, looking straight at me. I'd almost forgotten about my wish to find him, but there we were, at last, face to face. Mark Theo Stewart. *Was it a coincidence that his middle name was the male version of my first name?* As it happened, my mother's first name was my middle name. The answer to my seeking had lay hidden in my name the entire time. Joyce chuckled knowingly and said it was truly fitting. Nat had always been a prankster and good with words—a Scrabble wizard. Joyce seemed quietly disturbed that both her friends had lied to her about my parentage, and concluded our talk with, "I'm mad at them both, but I think it's quite obvious Nat chose your name carefully."

I easily tracked down Mark's wife of the last fifteen years. She was living in New Mexico and, after a quick search through the internet white pages, I was on the phone with her, sending shock waves through her being. She told me Mark had had many regrets during his dying days, and she was able to put all of them to rights before he died, except one. Thea. He regretted rejecting me and never taking an active part in my life or participating financially. He told his wife, Judy, that if I ever came calling to tell me that he was deeply sorry for his actions and that he loved me very much.

Judy was over the moon because now she felt Mark could finally be at peace—his last regret finally corrected. Judy's words were the last confirmation I needed to close that chapter of my life.

Death

Death is the great equalizer of life. Whether it be the death of a friend, pet, family member, or your disjointed Ego, you cannot hide from the truth of what death brings you: the instant insight that control is an illusion. Not once did you have control over any course of your life. You were in charge of making choices and changing your perspective, yes, but that was all.

Death is a great teacher, a master of awakening you to the ever-fluid nature of this reality. It teaches you to surrender, and quite harshly unmasks all pretenses of falsehood. To be truly comfortable in this world, you have to accept death. It is what awaits us all. In that way, death and birth are the greatest polarities of our existence. Opposite faces on the same coin. Ultimately, death is a real bummer for those left behind.

The first band I ever saw live in concert was The Police—Hamburg, 1983. I absolutely loved The Police. I wasn't the kind of teenage girl to have a poster of a band on her wall, but they were plastered all over my heart. The drummer was my first band-member crush ever—I was completely head over heels in love with his talent. I could listen to Stewart Copeland play drums for hours, even today.

Fast-forward to May 5, 2011. I was sitting in a café, working on my columns for Jacob, when the song "Message in a Bottle" came on. My awareness took me directly to the lyrics "…*sending out an SOS…*" I immediately felt that this was a smoke signal from Jacob. The last I'd heard, he was doing remarkably well, so I ignored the message and wrote it off as me making stuff up.

But before leaving the café, another song came on that washed over me like a tsunami. "*All my bags are packed, I'm ready to go, I'm standing here, outside your door, I hate to wake you up to say goodbye.*"

I looked around for some explanation, and my inner voice said, *If you ignore the message, I'll just send another.* I was packing up my belongings when the volume of the song seemed to increase, and I could no longer ignore it. *"...'Cause I'm leaving on a jet plane, don't know when I'll be back again."* The floodgates opened with an instant knowing.

The next day, May 6 according to my journal, I received a call from Vivian. Jacob was in the hospital in acute rejection. I had my confirmation and immediately went into tuning mode. I tuned Jacob, his liver, the room he was in, the doctors—you name it, I tuned it. But nothing seemed to work. I emailed Deena and called Martina. *What was I doing wrong?* Both of them spoke at length about how I needed to start the process of letting him go. That maybe it was not about trying to keep him here, but rather about holding a loving space for him to die. Accepting that he was in the process of transitioning and tuning, instead, for a peaceful passage.

Not what I wanted to hear.

Jacob's process of dying began when the doctors deemed him inoperable for another transplant because of an E. coli infection he'd contracted. The doctors estimated that his liver would last another week, but that it would take two weeks for the E. coli infection to clear up. The math didn't add up to another chance.

This news sent shock waves throughout his family. People deal with the end of life of a loved one in a multitude of ways. Some face it head-on, others hide, and some people just need time to come to grips. There is no right or wrong way to deal with the dying process; it's difficult no matter who you are.

I sought guidance on several occasions at the Spiritual Care Centre and consulted with the spiritual care specialist Daniel. His compassionate nature and professional reflections were very helpful. He recommended I be honest and open with Jacob and share any feelings or thoughts with him now, before he was moved to the palliative care floor. If you're going through a similar situation or know someone who is, I highly recommend these two books: *Being with Dying* by Joan Halifax and *Final Gifts* by Maggie Callanan and Patricia Kelley.

For the next three weeks, I went to hospital every morning to see Jacob after day care drop-off. Vivian was doing long hours at the hospital at this point, so this gave her some respite. This was my first intimate rendezvous with death, and I had no idea how to behave.

At first, I just acted like everything was normal. I rambled on and fidgeted with things in the room—my nervous energy ran away with itself. Then, as Jacob became weaker and weaker, the lulls became longer and longer.

Silence.

This was uncomfortable at first. And then the stillness became a blessing. An opportunity for deep listening.

It became obvious to me that there was absolutely nothing for me to do. All I could do was hold a loving space for Jacob in the silence. To be there with him, hold his hand, and tell him I loved him. To listen to the unspoken messages in the humbling hush. To speak with him, Soul to Soul.

Wise silence.

From this silence I learned that I had unspoken sentiments I wished to express to Jacob. I fumbled about in the metaphorical dark, trying to find words to express my feelings. To declare them verbally meant I would have to feel them, and I was trying to hold it all together for Jacob. But time was of the essence and, thanks to Daniel, I pulled out my bag of brave and wrote my thoughts on a piece of paper:

"You were a perfect stranger when I first met you. Then you became less strange and more perfect. And then you became a friend. A very good friend. A less than strange, perfectly great friend.

Even when you were unwell and obviously suffering, you still found the energy to ask the right questions. To listen. To care. To share. And to make us all laugh.

You are a beautiful person. An inspiring friend. A person who gives and wishes nothing in return. You've been my greatest teacher. My greatest friend.

You changed my world. You inspired me to live my life with no regrets, to dare to do what I never thought I could: to follow my heart. To pursue my dreams and just be me. To shine and not be afraid to do so. You appreciate me just the way I am, with no expectations, forever guiding me on my journey with complete, unconditional understanding. For this amazing gift of love and friendship, I am forever grateful."

About a week before Jacob died, I held his hand and spoke these words with a weeping soul. I left his room that day flooded with tears as my heart cracked open. Jacob, in all his love and support for me, had penetrated the protective fortress I'd spent my life building around myself, and it all came crashing down. I was vulnerable and scared out of my wits, but Jacob was showing me that, no matter what the external world had taught me, there was nothing to be afraid of; love was not to be feared, just embraced. Fear was nothing but a pirate that had ravaged my ship. It was time for me to salvage what I could from the wreckage.

After that, I sat with Jacob in unconditional quietude. I understood that there was nothing for me to do but be still. To share the tranquil stillness with him. It takes time to befriend the whispering voice within and to listen—deeply—to the unspoken boundless connection between Souls. As much as Jacob did not want "…a truck with death…"[2] his road there was well underway. I did not have time to idle in this learning. I tuned into the sharp silence and turned up the volume. This

---

[2] From Pablo Neruda's poem "Keeping Quiet."

profound connection was a parting gift from my dear friend that shifted my awareness inward. A skill I use every day.

Our Western culture does not value silence. There is always chatter somewhere, whether it is billboards flashing, the car radio blaring, the TV blabbering, social media pings, or even our own minds. Everywhere we go, there is noise. Some people can't stand the silence and turn the TV on for company. Each to their own, but I learned from my time with Jacob that silence is very powerful. It centres you in the moment. It awakens you, like death, to the true nature of reality. It forces you to stop thinking, and after a while, the mind chatter dissipates. You simply are. Nothing more than patternings of motion. All connected. All one. A collective soup of creative consciousness connected through threads of love.

Before he died, Jacob shared my short passage with Vivian, and together they decided it would be fitting for the rabbi to read my words at his funeral. I remember being seated in the second-to-last row amongst a sea of people I didn't know when the rabbi spoke my personal thoughts. I blushed at the honour of my words being exposed and felt immense gratitude.

The day of his birth ended up being shared with the day of his funeral. *Were we meant to laugh or cry?* Life is cruel in its ironies. The polarities of life were ever apparent once again. Motion rest, high low, peace chaos, sunrise sunset.

Two days after the funeral, my son and I headed to the backyard to get the car. We were about to get in when a golden retriever appeared out of thin air. My son looked at me, perplexed. "Where'd he come from?" I shook my head, just as bewildered as he was. There was something so familiar about this dog. I looked at the energetic beauty and, oddly enough, heard myself say, "Jacob?" My son looked at me curiously. The dog barked at us and bounced around playfully. I opened the car door for my son and looked back—the dog had vanished. I rushed into the laneway to see where he'd gone, but there was no sign of him. I assumed my grief was getting the best of me.

The following night, we had our customary Sunday dinner with the family. It was the usual gathering, and my family extended their sympathies to me. My niece asked who had died, and I told her a dear friend named "Jacob." She jumped out of her seat and yelled, "Jacob!" Before anyone knew why she was so excited, she darted out of the room and up to her bedroom. She returned lickety-split with a children's book in her hand. She pointed to the title page and smiled proudly. "Jacob." I looked down at the cover. A golden retriever dog was running along a beach, and the title was *Brave Jacob*. Both my son and I looked at the cover in silence. My niece began to summarize the story with great zeal; *Jacob, a blind golden retriever, saves a girl from drowning in the ocean*. My son was the only other person present who understood why this was so meaningful. We exchanged a look of acknowledgment.

In case that was not confirmation enough, the very next day, my friend Martina called me to tell me that her friend Monica, a medium in Manitoba, had called her that morning and told her that someone named "Jacob" wanted to say hello and that Martina would understand. After that, I never doubted my intuition again, whether I thought a dog was talking to me or a tree.

We always have the choice to conceal or reveal ourselves. I had, for the better part of my life, chosen to conceal my true self from the world and from people. But Jacob, in life and death, reminded me that sharing your authentic self is truly a wonderful gift.

For all my insight and gratitude for the experience, I did struggle greatly to deal with my grief. So I channeled it into several creative endeavours: a children's book on grief and loss, dedicated to Jacob's young nephew, Yves, and a twelve-week hospice training programme, which allowed me to volunteer at a child-focused respite and palliative care centre.

Several months later, thanks to a good friend, my children's book was picked up by a children's publisher for international distribution.

The Burn

As I continued to move forward towards resonance with the Divine within, it became obvious that I had some other buried traumas my body wanted to be free of, namely anxiety and panic. One weekend when my ex had arrived for his time with our son, I drove about three and half hours outside Vancouver to indulge in a weekend of sleeping in, massages, and long walks in the forest. But the farther away from the city I drove, the more aware I became of an unsettled feeling spreading throughout my body. I had no words to describe this new feeling at the time. I thought maybe I was coming down with the flu.

I finally arrived, tires crunching on the icy snow, eager to take a bath and soothe my tenderness.

The hotel was dimly lit. I saw people off in a dining room, eating and chatting. They looked up at me and smiled. Suddenly, I was launched back to my early years as a toddler. Strange, unknown faces looking at me in the dark. My body immediately went into panic. My palms became moist, and I started looking around for an escape. But no one was familiar, and I felt so alone and terrified. The receptionist arrived in the shadowy David Lynch–like lighting, and smiled to welcome me.

I immediately asked if there was a nurse or doctor on staff and was told that the nearest hospital was a two-minute drive. At this point, my heart was racing, and I was in full-blown panic. I started my pranayama breathing and talked myself into some form of calm while driving to the hospital. When I arrived, I was told to sit, and wait.

Desperate, I dialed my mom. The second she answered, I spilled my panic into the phone.

Her voice was calm and reassuring as she asked me the most important question, "What do you need me to do?"

In that moment, I broke down and cried a torrent of tears. I understood that inside, her question was my answer. My feelings of safety and being loved unconditionally were at play. I asked her if she would come and get me.

She replied without hesitation. "Of course, your father and I are leaving right away." At that point, the doctor was ready to see me, and within minutes, I was given Ativan to quiet my alarm.

I fell asleep, soothed by the notion that my parents were there for me. Their coming to get me was the sign of unconditional love, the link of connectivity I needed, to allow the panic to pass through me. Because now, as opposed to when I was one or two years old, I had a stable family that *was* there for me no matter what the circumstances.

It was some months later I learned that, at the age of two, I'd been taken by my biological mother's common-law partner on a plane to California. On the flight home, the plane had some technical difficulties and made an emergency landing in a cornfield. There was sheer panic in the plane as people scrambled to get out. Unknown faces in the dark that could not console me. *Where was Mamma?*

At my young age of two, I absorbed every ounce of terror and panic on that plane into my unconscious, feeling body. It was too much for my little being to assimilate, so I buried that distressing experience until I was forty years old and balanced enough to feel it, push through, and release it.

I realised that the way to real resonance with my inner being was to release all negative emotions, and that included past traumas that were tucked away in the treasure chest lost somewhere at emotional sea. Lost, but not completely forgotten, or processed.

The body wants to push the negative emotions and trauma up and out of its system, and when it does, it can cause real discomfort, fear, and sometimes panic/terror because we relive the original emotions. It's important that we allow these unresolved emotions to pass through us, so that we can then release them from our emotional memory and body. Everyone is different, and how you move through this will be very specific to you. Seek professional counsel in the area of trauma if you need help to move through it.

These are unique experiences to me and will not be the same for you. However, what will be the same as you raise your vibration to meet your higher consciousness is your body's urge to clean house. It will bring unmatched frequencies of lower resonance up and out of you. I call it the "prescribed burn," just like what farmers do to improve the health of their fields. You allow these negative experiences to burn through you, and, in so doing, you release them and leave a healthier energetic field behind.

Every feeling you have, positive or negative, affects your cells somewhere in the intricate apparatus of your body. Your cells then have a power of influence over their neighbouring cells, and so positive or negative vibrations are sent out like a ripple in a pond. The cells of your body instinctively know how to be *well*. However, if you flood your body-system with negative attitudes and bad vibrational patterning, such as stress or anger, you will influence your cellular structure in an unfavourable way.

With a positive shift in perspective, the obvious happens— change. Suddenly, you are dropping old habits, and when you do, you transform more things in your life, and then more reshaping perpetuates more expansion, and it's a ripple effect that never seems to end. Change of any significant kind really is an inside job, and it is my belief that it's impossible to divorce your health from your emotions.

It definitely takes time to adjust to letting go of the illusion that you are in control and to stop resisting your true potential. It's a never-ending cha-cha-cha of almost blind faith into the unknown.

CHAPTER FIVE

2011–2015

"The fool who persists in his folly will become wise."

—William Blake

Grandma Gordon was a woman ahead of her time and one of my favourite people in this lifetime. She never judged me and, although she had the gift of the gab, she also had the ability to listen. I think the quality I liked most about Grandma was the *what-you-see-is-what-you-get*. She taught swimming at the YWCA and pioneered learn-to-swim and water safety classes her entire life, when it was not yet fashionable to be a working mother. She had her third child in her forties in the mid '60s when it was anything but the norm. She was an outstanding trick water-skier, and put on an astonishing show well into her sixties. I would watch her from the back of the boat and secretly think, *Is she superhuman?*

She'd start waterskiing with two skis and then take one off and ski with it over her head, while holding on with only one hand. Then she'd drop the ski and slalom on one ski, submitting to the tug of the boat, swooping back and forth across the waves effortlessly. She'd then come back to centre and do a 180-degree turn and ski backwards. And if that wasn't enough, she'd lift one leg into the hand grip and ski slalom with no hands!

Even after my grandpa died, Grandma wasn't one to sit

around and wallow. She dated well into her eighties and was active in her community. She went dancing every Friday night, played golf, and never shied away from a long walk in -35C. I remember how she put us all to shame at my sister's wedding, kicking off her shoes and dancing a hole in the floor.

Swimming, the water, teaching, dancing—that was her resonant nature.

Grandma always told me about the first time she saw me. I'd been adopted only months earlier, and we drove to Edmonton to visit my mom's folks. Grandma said she could still remember the moment I got out of the car. She described me as "bright as a button" and remembered how my face lit up when I saw the choo-choo train birthday cake she'd purchased for me. On subsequent birthdays, she'd send me one of those Hallmark cards, "You're such a precious granddaughter, a treasure from above, a little ray of sunshine filled with happiness and love," with a handwritten letter and a check for twenty-five dollars. Always twenty-five dollars. Didn't matter that the cost of living went up over the years, she was consistent. When I called her, she always answered with an excited, "Hi sweet pea, so lovely to hear your voice." We had a rare connection from day one, and she always made me feel special and appreciated.

In the years during my greatest contrast with my dad, Grandma was a person I could lean on. She would remind me that I should not live my life for anyone else, and that, when all was said and done, *your dad is a good, hardworking man*. She always reassured me that, in the end, it wouldn't matter, and the tension would all be forgotten. My fondest memory of Grandma is sitting at the end of the dock at the lake, watching the sun set together. She drank Kahlúa, and I had ice-tea. We gabbed all night until the feasting mosquitos were unbearable.

It was no surprise to me that about two weeks before my grandma passed, I started to smell her everywhere. One day, I was in my garden pulling weeds, and her smell simply wafted over me. I looked around, and of course she was not there, but her essence was everywhere. I smiled and said hello and just got on with my day. Then, about one week later, after putting my son to bed, I was reading a book and sipping my nightly tea, when her fragrance became very noticeable. I closed my eyes and tuned in. *Did she need something?*

In a space I can only describe as neither here nor there, a sort of in-between-worlds place, I met her. She seemed excited and we hung out for a long while. She let me know that she would be leaving soon, but that a spark of her Soul would always remain with me. We enjoyed that space together like those long sunsets at the lake, until we were interrupted by my son calling me from the top of the stairs. I hugged her spirit goodbye and felt her energy slipping away. I was about to well up when my son called for me again. I promptly broke the connection and went upstairs.

Two weeks later, the day after my son and I arrived in Gothenburg for a holiday, I got a call from my mom saying that Grandma had passed away during the night. My number-one fan and superhuman trick skier had crossed over. The grief engulfed me, and I cried for hours, but we were on vacation, and Grandma would have wanted us to continue our adventure. And so, instead of trying to get to Edmonton in time for her funeral, we said our goodbyes with our own ceremony near the element she loved so much, the water.

Tightness vs Lightness of Being

The Fool in the tarot represents the Self, and she knows life is a game, a play, a labyrinth, and participates with complete innocence and abandon. She takes a leap of faith with only a few belongings and her faithful dog, and in complete trust and surrender, she ventures forth into the unknown. But by persisting in her folly, at the end of her journey, and the tarot, the Fool reaches paradise regained with the World card.

We are all just fools in this play of life, and as the final curtain fell on my grandmother's incredible production, I was once again reminded that death is simply the interval between a purely conscious existence and a human, body-bound existence. I inwardly wondered what incredible things my grandma would do in her next lifetime. *Would she be male or female? Would I have the pleasure of meeting her again, albeit as a different character?*

I believe we are all born with a pure connection to the great creative intelligent source I like to call the Boundless Core of All Consciousness. We come into this world as an expression of this creative intelligence. Our parents/guardians (if they are not in tune with their inner greatness), schools, teachers, religion, society, and our unconscious culture train us and our Ego to be out of resonance with our inner deeper knowing. They try and define us and design us to have certain responses to stimuli, and over time, we slowly create self-limiting biases about ourselves and the world at large. We become disconnected from our limitless being and the total existing Universe. We begin looking at life through an unconscious, disempowered lens. Then, one of two things happens: Something shifts inside of us, usually because of an outside stimulus (event, book, film, death, birth, song, near-death experience, person) which changes our perspective and teases our awakening, or we continue along the path of non-resonant vibration and never pull out of the programming of fear and control. As Confucius said, "A man who understands the Tao (the Course of Nature) in the morning may die with no regrets in the evening."

My son is a young teenager now and going to an international school in a foreign country. He is surrounded by kids from other cultures and is being taught open-mindedness, resilience, and flexibility simply by being in this setting. I try to cultivate and support him in his choices and bring nonconformist ideas to him at home through discussion, books, and films, but I never force any dogma or religion on him. At a very young age, he said the school system was teaching useless information and was generally a waste of his time. He was adamant that learning was important, but that kids needed to learn skills and take subjects that allowed them to be themselves and thrive in the world. He wanted a school that would allow him to align with who he was and give him the skill sets to do so.

I don't completely disagree with him, and I am now researching schools that would allow him to do just that. In his particular case, it has to be a school that cultivates his growth as a footballer (soccer player) and possibly as a coach, all while preparing him for the framework of our world through more traditional subjects. For all I know, he may grow up to play a part in changing our current educational system. As a parent, I'm simply trying to follow his cues and give him the best opportunities I can. I am, however, not perfect, and like all parents, I make mistakes every day.

Sadhguru, yogi and mystic, once said, "A child is not a legacy. It is a life." I have never encouraged or even suggested that my son follow in my footsteps. *Why would I?* He's an incredible individual who will grace our world in his unique spirit, and already does so every day. I often wonder why parents want their kids to do as they do, or why they prescribe a certain profession to them before they've even reached grade four. *What purpose does that serve?* Maybe it feeds their disconnected Ego with the fantasy of recognition or approval. What it does do is keep their kids in the compulsive, repetitive cycle like the old hamster. Let them choose and discover for themselves. Let them blossom into the expression that is individual to them. Oscar Wilde once said, "To live is the rarest thing in the world. Most people exist, that is all."

Many of us exist in the unconscious realm unaware that

there is so much more to tap into. If I hadn't embarked on a path of self-discovery after giving birth to my son, like so many, I would have no clue today that I was living unconsciously and advocating 95 percent of my time for an uncreative, conformist narrative. That I was in fact imposing my will on the world, as opposed to co-creating with it. We don't ride the magic carpet alone; we co-create it with our Soul-self.

From my current place of understanding, I believe there are four lanes we can travel: the *unconscious* lane, the *conscious* lane, the *aware* lane, and the *inter-dimensional, quantum* lane. I believe you can be unconscious yet aware, conscious and inter-dimensional, but not both unconscious and conscious. As far as I can tell from my own experiences, they preclude each other; you simply cannot be conscious and unconscious at the same time.

However, we don't know what we don't know, and I, for one, am very open to the idea that there may be another lane, or two, or three that will be brought into our awareness at some later point in time. *What lies beyond quantum and inter-dimensional?*

Both Jacob and Grandma convinced me, in different ways, that just because most humans dance to a repeating record of hard logic and precision, it didn't mean I had to. Jacob cautioned me once, quoting Socrates, "Beware of the barrenness of a busy life." All too often, we get lost in the pretense of being busy, believing it means accomplishment of some kind. *Yet, in all our busyness, what exactly are we achieving?* It's nothing but a delay tactic, an avoidance mechanism, so we don't have to do the work of looking at ourselves and owning our shadow aspects. It's been said that people who have nothing to do become busybodies. We'd all be much better off meditating, taking a nap, cooking, or staring out into space for several hours than wasting hours shopping for a bargain deal or pretending all our "busyness" is actually productive in some way.

We've been enchanted with the idea that busy means productive and productive means accomplished and accomplished means successful. It's an illusion, of course. It all depends on how you decide to measure your own success and worth. I call it the "*tightness of being*" as opposed to the "*lightness of being.*" The *tightness of being* is grounded in the devouring abstractions of fame, money, self-importance, and the cultivated ignorance of the illusion, whereas the *lightness of being* is connected to the centre of our authentic Soul-self, the Divine within. One speeds you up with external, illusory constructs, and the other slows you down to the speed of your inner voice and wisdom.

I was talking with a dear friend not long ago who was dizzy from all the busy and basically had to take time off because of burnout. She admitted she felt guilty sitting at home doing nothing or taking a nap midday. *Was that not a sign of an unsuccessful, lazy, good-for-nothing person?* she asked. I shared this quote with her from the writings of Sir John Lubbock.

> Rest is not idleness, and to lie sometimes on
> the grass on a summer's day listening to the
> murmur for the water, or watching the clouds
> float across the sky, is hardly a waste of time.

We talked a lot about self-care, and I told her that napping almost daily was a simple way for me to switch off and reenergize. She glared at me, somewhat horrified. I told her it was part of what had allowed me to be hugely successful. Her eye twitched in a seizure of bewilderment because in her mind I was not successful in any way that warranted my saying so.

She cautiously asked *how* I'd been successful, when I was not getting paid for anything I was creating. There it was, like a bright red balloon in a white room. A hypnotized, critical mindset. I popped her bubble and told her I was hugely prosperous unto myself and that I did not need validation from the outside world to make me feel or believe I was successful. I knew what I'd created was of immense value to me, and that was all that really mattered. If you measure your worth and success against those around you, you're setting yourself up for feeling worthless every time. The writing of this book is a big win for me personally. Whether it sells one copy, no copies, or a billion, is of no consequence. The success is in the creation of it. Connection, love, growth, and co-creation were the point, not the outcome.

Within fourteen months, I'd lost two very significant people in my life, both of whom inspired me to express myself unapologetically and stop being spell-bound by the cultivated ignorance all around me. I was inspired to play an active part in my own salvation, in the quest for self-love and self-expression.

I yearned to leave the unconscious, default settings of the rat race behind and cultivate my authentic, imperfect self, and find clarity in my purpose. As I reevaluated my career and looked for other ways to create and express myself, I became aware that it was in the stillness that I might find answers. I stopped the pointless busyness in my life that was leading nowhere and consciously dedicated my time to figuring out what the second act of my *Life* was going to be.

Hawaii

My grandma vacationed in Hawaii with my grandpa several times during her lifetime. One of my favourite pictures of the two of them was taken there—it captures singing eyes and easy smiles, leathery sun-soaked skin, and vibrant leis. An air of effortless existence spills from that photo and always makes me want to set sail for those distant islands.

My newfound connection with dolphins led me to a website

of a woman who gave seminars and led swims with dolphins in open water on the Big Island. I was able to arrange for my ex to stay with our son, and I signed up for a one-week adventure.

Dolphins are incredibly curious and playful creatures. They come into the warm bays of the Hawaiian Islands in the morning to rest after evenings of feeding. We saw many pods of dolphins gliding in resting mode every day we went out. One afternoon, with a few new friends from the previous week's seminar, we went to the Ho'okena beach to snorkel. We'd heard that spinner dolphins were frequently spotted swimming close to the beach. Sprinting across the scorching lava sand, we found immediate relief in the clear water caressing the shore and slipped into the turquoise ocean, eager to explore the expanse with our oceanic friends. We began to navigate the underwater world below and, within fifteen minutes, were swimming eye to eye with a few playful spinners.

One particularly spirited dolphin invited me to play the "leaf" game with her. This is quite a common pastime between dolphin and human, but it was my first time, and I was utterly delighted. The dolphin swam by me with some sort of yellow green foliage wrapped around her pectoral fin. She then dove down and released the leaf. She spun out of my way and eagerly watched as I kicked furiously to catch the sinking leaf. I grabbed it and pumped my way back to the surface in victory. I caught my breath and descended below the surface again—all while my friend waited impatiently for me, like a dog about to fetch a ball. I torpedoed down as fast as I could and released the leaf. The spinner's eyes filled with delight as she watched the leaf float like a feather further and further down into the big blue. She then pumped her tail and dashed down to sweep the leaf up with her pectoral fin. She speedily swam back to me to show me she'd retrieved the prize. She then plunged down and released the leaf. My turn.

We played this game for a long frolicsome spell of time. I

Petrified Forest

One day, while still on the Big Island, one of my new friends from the seminar, César, and I decided to visit the petroglyph park. He questioned me in a thick, Javier Bardem accent, "Petrohips?" But I waved him to the car and reassured him it would be fun, and we drove off, leaving the rainbows and fairy-tale hills of Waimea behind us.

By the time we hit the west coast, it was scorching hot, and the wind was gusting. With the windows down and hair swirling like candy canes, we sang along to the local reggae tunes until we reached the petroglyph park.

Many years earlier, in 2000, while in Cozumel taking my scuba license, I went into a tattoo shop and got my first tattoo. It was odd because I had never wanted to get a tattoo, but there I was, looking at the artist's book of drawings. I pointed to a stick figure and propped my ankle up. "Right there, please." I didn't even know what the stick figure was, I just knew I wanted to have it on my body. As I walked up the pathway towards the petroglyphs, suddenly I became aware of my tattoo. I showed César the little stick figure, and he smiled: "I bet we find same figure here today." I got the goosies, which reassured me that we would.

As we headed towards the outdoor museum, I looked up and became aware of a cloud above us in the sky. It was really windy, and yet this cloud was not moving.

César and I walked together in the first circle of boulders, looking at the various figures; some looked like they were hunting, some fishing, and others surfing. We then headed down a winding path covered by ash-coloured trees. It was as if a river of lava had run through a forest, leaving nothing but bent-over trees and magma sand in its wake. As I walked farther into the dense tunnel of branches, I felt suddenly protected and watched.

I whispered *hello* in my head and looked above me. Something caught my eye up in the trees. A little face. I smiled, happy for the confirmation. I automatically went for my iPhone to take a picture, and then suddenly reminded myself of my manners. *May I take pictures?* The answer was very clear and undeniable: *No.* I nodded and was so glad I'd asked. I thanked them for showing themselves to me and continued to walk ahead. I was happy to interface with these beings and, through the purity of my thoughts, I let them know my purpose was peaceful. I asked if they would tell me a little bit about themselves. They responded and, although cautious, they did seem eager. I felt the conversation spread from my head to my heart, and I opened myself to receive whatever information they wished to share. I was quickly filled with images and a sense of unconditional love similar to when I'd been swimming with the dolphins. My eyes swelled with a salty surf as I felt their gentleness all around me. They showed me their small stature and how very fluid and agile they were in the trees. They were soulful and expressive. They informed me telepathically that they were protecting the area because of the glyphs.

I looked beyond the trees for my cloud, and, sure enough, with a determined Mona Lisa effect, it continued to follow me in the petroglyph park.

César was nowhere to been found, and I suddenly felt drawn to walk ahead a little more briskly. The concept of time seemed to disappear, as it had done underwater. I really couldn't tell you how long I was in the park area, although it felt like a lifetime. There were many times I wished I could have stayed forever. It felt like home. I slowed my pace slightly and looked around. I heard what sounded like a bird of some kind, calling in the trees. I felt guided to follow it—which meant going off the trail. The sign at the entrance of the park was quite clear: Do Not Leave the Trail at Any Time. But I trusted my sprightly friends. The song continued to lead me until I was in front of a huge cave. Up behind it were some smaller caves. The tune indicated that this was where I should go. I also understood that this was their home or dwelling.

I climbed through the very thorny brush, following their melody, and again, thanked them for inviting me to their home. A river of tears traced down my face as I felt their welcoming tenderness around me. I stood there, completely invisible from the trail. I sat down for a while and just opened my heart and sat peacefully in their presence. They told me to drink more water. I was very dehydrated. The black magma sand under my feet was soaking the water from my body like a sponge.

I sat for a long while, and in my head asked them how tall they were. I didn't get a response and wondered if I should have asked a more tantalizing question. After a long while, I had the impulse to walk over to another spot. I stood there, not knowing what I was doing. Then, I looked down. Right there, at my feet, was a little piece of poo. I looked at it curiously and inwardly chuckled. They were giving me confirmation of their size. I deducted, based on the size of my dog's poo (a ten-kilogram rescue from Santiago) that these beings could not be much bigger than two to three feet tall and must weigh approximately three to six kilograms. I thanked them again for sharing this detail with me. They pointed out gleefully that this flawless artifact was picture ready. I joined in their playful temperament and captured the little log with one click.

I headed back to the trail and noticed the cloud, still steady in the sky above me. I found César lying on the ground in front of a large piece of coral, and I left him to his peacefulness and continued along the trail. It was blisteringly hot now, and I had two sips of water left. Suddenly, a dragonfly appeared and circled around my head a few times. Go back. I ignored it and continued on. I was so determined to find the same petroglyph I had tattooed on my ankle, so I stubbornly pushed forward. But, thankfully, the dragonfly came back and fluttered around my head one more time. This time, I listened to the gentle guidance and headed back the way I came.

Above me, in the clear sky, hung my cloud—motionless like a suspended mobile over a baby's crib. Suddenly, in my mind's eye, I saw a flower: a beautiful rose. I heard that my new friends were going to give me a flower as a parting gift. I looked around at the petrified scenery of barren bark and ash, and said out loud, *"A flower? Here?"* I assumed the flower I saw in my mind's eye *was* the gift, and I thanked them.

As I got closer to the main part of the park, I noticed another tourist looking down at a rather large boulder. I hadn't noticed it earlier. After she left, I went over to the big rock, and sure enough, as César had predicted, engraved on the large slab was the very same petroglyph I had tattooed on my ankle. I was thrilled to bits. César clicked a few pics on my iPhone to capture the likeness of the two sketches.

I then led César off the trail to the cave I'd discovered earlier. He was immediately enchanted by it and crawled into the dark, dusty cavity without hesitation. I sat in front of the opening and continued to wilt in the heat. César emerged some time later, covered in a brownish-grey dust from head to toe. Had it been two hours or two minutes? My sense of time was so strange in that place, I really couldn't be sure. He told me of a very large spider he met and an opening he'd found. From my vantage point, you could see no light in the cave, but on the other side of it, there was opening at the top. And then he held his hand out and said, "This is for you." He opened his hand and there in his palm was a dainty, delicate, brown flower that looked like a rose. I was speechless. I had not told him of my *conversations* with the beings of the park or the dragonfly. I couldn't believe how beautiful it was. I didn't have a chance to become emotional because I was too amazed. It was confirmation that what I was experiencing were not just silly imaginings in my mind. The flower was evidence, if you will, that I was having a trans-dimensional experience. I was profoundly moved by their gesture and thanked them profusely for the gift. I keep the flower by my bed, in a special container for safekeeping.

I honoured their existence while expressing my gratitude for welcoming me. A swell of unconditional love flooded my being, and a stream of joy trickled from my eyes. I stood for a long spell simply being in the surge of fondness and enchantment with them. My mind began to try and quantify the unquantifiable. I told it to relax and dispense with the need to assess and appraise. I was so immersed in the moment I didn't want any interruptions as I sank deeper into the wonderment. I was so engrossed in the grand, synergistic unfolding of interconnectedness with the imponderable. My familiar narratives were being pushed aside to make way for this new landscape. A mysterious place beyond the visible. I was in euphoric flow, giddy like a child in fantastical imaginings.

Quite reluctantly, I came back to the familiar backdrop of my recognizable world and said farewell to what felt like close family. I felt the presence of these beings all around us as we headed back to the entrance. They escorted us along the trail up until a certain point, and then I felt them hang back. I passed through a wave of dynamic energy. It glimmered in my peripheral vision and seemed to be a bubble or field of some kind. I turned and bowed slightly in gratitude for their warm reception and generosity. I felt a gush of joyous sadness swell in my heart as I turned and walked away. As we exited the park, I looked up to see my steady-floating cloud had finally begun to move and change shape.

I immediately became cognizant that the construct of time does not exist within that energetic dome. I looked down at my hands to see if they had aged a hundred years, but no, I was still the same, physically.

As I walked out of the park and to the car, my iPhone pinged continuously, like Morse code. Missed messages and multiple calls. I saw the time and realised I'd been in the park for over four hours. I was expected to call home at three but had all but forgotten. Although my senses in the park were heightened and my awareness was keen, I'd experienced a kind of temporary amnesia. Lost in a sort of pure state of enthrallment, I had an experience beyond the doors of normal perception, swooning into the mysterious beyond and completely dispensing with my world of the here and now. I had travelled into the forever flow of an unscripted, inter-dimensional reality and had communicated and exchanged gifts, tangible and mysterious. I felt like an elk who had sprouted inter-dimensional antlers.

As we drove home, I pondered my purpose. If "we become what we behold" as Terence McKenna says, what did this mean for me personally? I considered my perceptual expansion and ability to tap into inter-dimensional and mysterious worlds. *Was I trying to conjure these unknowable worlds into my reality as a way to challenge science and my familiar narratives?*

My petrified-forest bathing was nothing less than mind-expanding and heart-opening. My being had been caressed by the infinite, the unknowable, by an expansive perception so great that time seemed to warp. I had left the rational behind and given myself over entirely to other realms and ecstasy.

I hope in disclosing my experience with you that it will help to remove the taboo so that others will be less secretive about their psychic and trans-dimensional encounters. I know I am not alone in my experiences. Let's shift our infant sensitivity about all things otherworldly and alien into a new place of acceptance and open-mindedness.

Gentle Giants

A year later, an invitation to an unexpected adventure arrived in my inbox. Come swim with the humpbacks in the wild! *What?! Was that even possible?* I'd always been fascinated with whales, and to swim with one was a bucket-list dream I never thought I'd realise. The invitation was from one of my Hawaiian buddies and I immediately began looking into the logistics of it. *Did I have the money? Could my ex stay with our son? Was I brave enough?*

Five months later, I found myself standing on a pier, getting my picture taken in front of the boat that would take us nine hours out to open ocean. We were headed to an area off the coast of the Dominican Republic that is known to be the largest breeding ground for the North Atlantic humpback whale.

I'd spent much of my childhood on a sailboat, so I was at ease with the swell of the sea. However, the crew insisted that even the most experienced sailors tended to get seasick on this particular ocean passage, and they recommended taking medicine. I didn't have any, so my cabinmate gave me some of hers. It knocked me out like a baseball bat, and I had absolutely zero recollection of our extremely rough crossing.

The boat dropped anchor for the week on the shoreless ocean. Twice a day, we chartered off in the little tender boats, searching for calm humpback whales to swim with. Our experienced guides used respectful approach techniques, and our group of eight would quietly slip into the water and glide alongside these gentle giants at a safe distance. I remember the first time I slid into their home and saw a humpback whale swimming only meters away. I lifted my head out of the water and looked around as if to say to someone, *Is this for real?* It was akin to the out-of-body experience I'd had years earlier; the same rush of excitement and thrill pulsed through my veins. I promptly put my snorkel back on. Humpbacks move quickly, even when only drifting, so you have to kick considerably to keep up. I didn't want to miss the wonder, so I swiftly fluttered my way back to the action.

By day three, we all felt like mermaids. After a hearty breakfast, we enthusiastically climbed into the tenders and attentively scanned the horizon for a flash of a tail or a misty spout of water. We swam with whales on every single trip out except for one. The whales we came across that afternoon were a competitive, "rowdy" group. In this breeding ground, the males come to find a mate, and on this particular day, there was a receptive female in the area and three males fighting it out for dominance. Rowdy groups give heavy-weight fighting a whole new meaning. These males will ram each other, hit each other with their pectoral fins, sometimes even hold one another under the water in an attempt to literally drown the competition. It's very physical, and the more participants, the more dramatic the show. We were kept at a safe distance in the boats but had ringside seats to the thrashing spectacle all the same. In the end, one male came out victorious and swam off with the female.

In the evenings, following a marvelous meal and many shared stories of the day's encounters, we convened on the upper deck to watch the sun set. In a gathered quiet, we observed as the sun hit the ocean's surface on the horizon and, in a quick flash of green, disappeared until the next morning.

On the last day, our boat captain dropped his hydrophone into the water and listened for whales. His face lit up with a birthday smile—today was our lucky day. There was a singing whale nearby. He was able to get us very close to the whale, who was suspended in a vertical position. Nothing but a nebulous silhouette hanging like a pendant with no tether in the limitless depths of the ocean. His song reverberated through the water and into our bodies, plucking strings at our emotional core. Again, I felt that familiar sense of oneness with all things and was so profoundly recalibrated in that moment I began to sob in my snorkel. I had to come up for air. I wept in the essence of perfect knowing, in splendid connection and oneness. Connected through a frequency called love, we are all one and the same. The giant swells of the ocean cradled me back and forth like a mother rocking her babe.

This experience was another overview effect, not from space, as astronauts experience it, but of a world within a world. It was a new perspective; a boundless ocean mise-en-scène that freed me from the bondage of land and the cruelty of life. It freed me from the broadcast of my Ego and tuned me into the frequency of the whole, the sacred.

I finally stopped crying and floated effortlessly in the ocean-filled whale symphony, swept away by the infinite and all-knowing understanding that competes with no thing. I had temporarily lost sight of the illusion of separation and was in a blissful oneness with all. I floated, awestruck by this breathtaking rendezvous with majesty and greatness.

Interspecies connection is powerful and based on an exchange of feelings and energy alone. Swimming eye to eye with a whale completely entrances you in a suspended moment of timelessness. It's a meeting of Souls, an exchange of love and empathy in what seems to be an everlasting moment of infinite bliss.

Eternal. Magical.

For seven days, I surrendered myself to the ocean and the angels of the deep. My entire being was soaked in uncompromising love and warmth. Their limitless *Geist* caressed my heart, mind, body, and Soul in a way similar to those quiet nights when I was breast-feeding my baby. Nothing short of divine.

Validation Comes from Within

I returned home with a real sense of ease and surrender and began to allow myself to dream about my passion to write and direct. In the beginning of my directing career, I'd been swayed into commercials as a way to gain experience and make money. When my son was born, everything shifted. I just couldn't bring myself to direct ads that promoted sugary cereals to kids or other useless products to the public.

I tried my hand at portrait photography for a while and quickly learned that it was fun but not tickling my Soul's desire. I created a cooking show, but networks never picked it up. I created VOD (video on demand) content, but in the end, the supplier could only fund one episode. It was a very frustrating time, trying to redefine my career.

As I embarked on this do-what-I-love-make-no-money journey, it became very obvious very quickly that we would have to downsize. Our three-story, four-bedroom house had been purchased with the idea of a growing, working family, not a shrinking, unemployed one.

And so, in 2014, I decided to sell my house in downtown Vancouver. I launched myself into the very tedious process of purging and selling, cleaning and donating. I left items on the curb for the local hoarders and curious passers-by. Still, the house was overflowing like a bag of theatre popcorn. It was a never-ending and exhausting experience that didn't let up for weeks.

At some point, my father weighed in with his opinion about doing a third-floor renovation. He insisted that by adding a bathroom and walk-out balcony, it would raise the value of the house by about fifty thousand dollars. He knew I was strapped for cash with all that I was spending getting it ready for sale, so money was tight. He said not to sweat it because he would do the labor of installing the new hardwood floors and bathroom tile himself. He said he would cover the cost of materials, and that I could repay him when all was said and done.

Three things ran through my brain: First, my concern for my father's health. He was seventy-two years old at the time, and laying hardwood by yourself is definitely not sipping cocktails poolside. Second, I was concerned that, working on his own, even if I assisted the best I could, he would not have the reno done by our deadline. And third, the sheer delight that my dad would actually do this for me no strings attached. But I thanked him and declined what I thought to be a generous offer.

That night, he sent me an Excel worksheet with his numbers. I looked them over and again, thanked him, and turned his offer down again. He called me the next day and persisted to hound me on the financial benefits. Instead of getting x amount of dollars for the house, with the reno you'll get xx amount of dollars. I explained that I didn't think it was worth the work, stress, and all the time and effort that it would require. *Thank you, Dad, but no thank you.*

My dad then moved into his über-salesman, I-don't-take-no-for-an-answer mode. He came over to the house with his notes and numbers and sat me down. He explained it all over again, assuming I just hadn't understood the first time around. It was a very simple equation: time + materials + effort = 50K profit. Nothing too complicated; we've all seen those *Flip My House* shows on TV. I said, "No, thank you" again, and my dad just sat there—finally speechless. Something was really festering in that head of his, but at the time I had no idea what it was. He was looking in every dusty corner for some way to get me to see, not necessarily understand, but see his point. He could not comprehend that his health and my stress were more important to me than fifty thousand dollars. It didn't compute in his brain. Like a calculator, he was pure digits, no emotion.

The abstraction made sense to him, but was one that clearly had no value to me.

Finally, not having another angle, he asked if I had discussed my decision with my ex-husband. *Why would I? It's my house.* I could sense my dad was about to play the nasty card called "guilt." I'd been there with him many times before, and it was like smelling the rain before it pours. He just wasn't going to let up. Exhausted at the idea of going into a gaslighting battle with him, I caved and agreed to do it. I mentioned my concerns for his health and for my mom, who would not be thrilled to have him working at my place for eight-hour days for the next six weeks. He said he would take care of her. I felt an unnerving rumble in my tummy that indicated I shouldn't have given in to him. But it was too late; my dad was off to buy materials and eager to get things rolling.

The next day, he arrived with lumber and nail guns, saws and hammers, and we began a six-week period of mild torment together. I prepared lunch for us both, and following our soup and sandwiches, he pulled out his notes and showed me more numbers. At this point, I was thinking he had OCD or something because I'd seen those blasted numbers a bazillion times. He took me through the cost of lumber, nails, caulk, tile, and so on. Upon seeing the list of items and knowing how much work it was all going to be, my empathy suddenly kicked in and I suggested paying him a couple thousand dollars for all his effort. I really wanted to compensate him. He looked up at me with a cold glare and said: "Did you think I was going to do all of this for nothing? You'll pay me the twenty grand you owe me."

My heart sank like a galvanized steel anchor. Down… down…down…it went into the depths of my inner ocean, landed with a thud at the bottom of my gut, and just lay there.

Still. Lifeless.

I glared at my dad for an eternal, never-ending moment

of appall and shock. It was like looking at a Francis O'Toole painting; he was realistic, cold, and calculating, but was he real?

In that moment, everything became clear: his opportunistic nature and why he had been so persistent, and, more importantly, who my father truly was. I got it. I finally understood—some forty years late, maybe—but it resonated so clearly for me. He was embossed on the other side of my coin.

Life and people had stripped me bare—bare to the bone, right down to my Soul. My father was ultimately my greatest teacher in contrast. I didn't love him any less. In fact, it only made me respect the role he'd agreed to play in my life more. There was immense relief in this understanding.

A few weeks later, before our traditional family gathering on Sundays, I looked into his grey-hazel eyes and saw the Soul-self behind the Ego self, the soft, loving nature behind the veil of humanness. In an instant, I received a message: *Don't hate me, I'm only here to show you what you deserve. I do it for your growth. Seek not validation from me, for it is not there. Only you can be your own source of validation. I love you immensely.* And just like that, my father broke our gaze and washed back a glass of whiskey. I was suddenly struck by how contrasting the outer appearances of these human costumes and Earthly roles really are to our true, divine essence. And from that moment forward, I never sought validation or praise from my dad, or anyone else for that matter.

In my own life, I've been able to witness the unconscious conditioning and non-resonant Ego at play, in myself and in others. This last example is just one of many that displays my father's teaching (disguised as personal agenda), as well as my own disallowing, at work.

When we look beyond the surface of what is happening, and open ourselves up to *deep* listening, we may hear the sub-sub-sub-text of any situation, the real yearning of our heart and the teachings that are available to us. When you realise it's all coming from a place of love, always, then you can only try and understand how it could be of benefit to you. A wise woman once told me that everyone who comes into your life is one of the following, or all of them:

- a reflection of yourself (a mirror)
- a lesson you need to learn
- a gift

My takeaway from my experience with my dad was threefold. I became aware that something within me was out of whack if he was indeed a reflection, which he was. I didn't know then, but after years of therapy and self-searching, I came to understand that I, too, was wounded, and that if my Ego had been in resonance with my inner knowing, I never would have attracted such behaviour. Therein was my lesson. I needed to learn how I was like him and why. And that, ironically, was a gift. I chose to work on myself more, to descend a little deeper in the intricate labyrinth of my experiences, so I could become more aware of my unconscious patterns and align more with my higher consciousness. Lao Tzu once said, "If you do not change direction, you may end up where you are heading." That's what I did; I purposefully changed direction. I wanted clarity, and insight, and I wanted to feel more in sync with my authentic Soul-self.

Months after the dust settled, I began to notice ways in which my father showed his love. Cooking was definitely one way he shared his heart, always making my son his favourite blueberry cheesecake and BBQ ribs when we came to visit. Years later, my dad also made a few financial gestures towards me that warmed my heart. He, too, was growing and learning. As the saying goes, "Improved behaviour is the best apology." I gracefully accepted my dad's offer with a quiet knowing.

Soul Connection

I began to make note of where and when my energy was reciprocated, and in some cases, appreciated and celebrated. It was a revelation to me. I'd been refitted during my early childhood to accept some disempowering treatment and had little conscious awareness of it for what was the better part of my life. The more I leaned into wanting *all* of me to be welcomed and valued, the stronger the calling was to return to Sweden. I was drawn back because my friends there were a supportive tribe. They may not have completely understood the language of my Soul, but they were open-minded and inspiring.

Translating the language of your Soul is not easy, and finding people who will listen and not judge that language is liberating. The further outside the box of limited beliefs I went, the fewer people there seemed to be in my life. It was akin to climbing plateaus of a pyramid. At the base, there was a large surface area where the majority of people spent their time, but as I climbed the octaves of the great structure, fewer and fewer people appeared. The surface area at the top was smaller, but that was not the issue; people were not lining up to reach the higher plateaus of the pyramid. There was no queue at all. I met a few stragglers, sharing stories and asking for water after the long climb, but it wasn't bumper-to-bumper traffic.

One day, my son came home from school and declared, "School is a zoo, Mommy. I'd really like to go to a school with less kids, so I can actually learn something." I was shocked by his clarity of desire and immediately began looking into alternatives for him.

After coming up short locally, I decided to apply for a spot at an international school in Gothenburg. *Couldn't hurt—who knows where the wind will blow us?*

Meanwhile, my house sold, and I continued the search for a new, smaller home, but without luck.

Then, in early March, I received a letter from the school in Gothenburg informing me that my son had an offer of placement. If I wanted to secure his spot, I would need to let them know by the end of April.

By the middle of April, I was still no closer to finding a new home. A few interesting job opportunities in Gothenburg had come across my radar, but there was nothing written in stone at this point. I was going to have to make the decision based purely on intuition and gut feeling. I took time to seek guidance from within and calmed my monkey mind. In silence, I surrendered to pure presence and awareness. *What was in our best interests?* Later that evening, during my nightly scroll of mystical content on the internet, I found a poem with a timely message:

> There is a voice inside of you,
> That whispers all day long,
> "I feel that this is right for me, I know that
> this is wrong."
> No teacher, preacher, parent, friend
> Or wise man can decide
> What's right for you—just listen to
> The voice that speaks inside.

I could not deny that the feeling of moving back to Sweden felt "right," but my logical mind was interfering and insisting I needed hard evidence of a job or maybe even a work contract signed before moving. This was my conditioned upbringing swirling a tornado of confusion in my mind. It was a mighty force threatening to hurl me into that familiar narrative of limited consciousness. Its path of destruction was intent on swallowing me whole.

At this point, I'd moved all my furniture and belongings into storage, and my son and I were living out of suitcases at my parents' place. I had one week to let the school in Gothenburg know if we were accepting their offer of placement.

I awoke one morning with the Édith Piaf lyrics to "La Vie en Rose" flooding my awareness. My attention was drawn to Mr. True Love from Gothenburg, and delightful memories of our past affections saturated my being. I inwardly laughed at Spirit's use of my fond memories of this man as bait. Like dangling a carrot in front of the horse, Spirit was trying to coax me in a specific direction. Love is the most powerful motivating force, after all.

Later that day, while walking my dog, I saw an Ikea truck delivering a mattress to a neigbouring house. I smiled and insisted I needed a job, not just external signs.

Two days later, according to my journal, I received an email from an old friend who was working for a production/animation company. She insisted we Skype and talk job opportunities. Following our video chat, without her actually offering me a specific job, she insisted she would be able to get me a job once I was there.

I had three days until my son's spot at the school in Gothenburg would expire. Once again, I asked my inner guide for clarity.

After a morning frenzy of getting my son to school on time, I found myself having a late breakfast. My dad was drinking his coffee at the kitchen table and looking at his watch from time to time. I joined him, and we chatted about whether the US was ready for a female president and other news-related topics. Then the doorbell rang and, while I was midsentence, my dad declared, "Oh, he's here. That was great, I just wasted ten minutes waiting for him." He hastily got up and answered the door.

I promptly left the house and went to my special place. I leaned up against my favourite tree and relaxed into a meditative state, finding tranquility in the peaceful space within. I asked for clarity once again. I was shown an upside-down heart and reminded that no one will ever be able to validate me. Only I can validate myself. My inner knowing said that moving to Sweden would assist in my growth towards self-love. And the heart moved to an upright position. My inner voice pointed out that in my father's words there was a message for me: *I'm just wasting time.* I smiled.

That night, I awoke from a dream with these words piercing through me: *…you're on hyperdrive to Soul fulfillment.*

The next morning, I called the school in Gothenburg and accepted their offer of placement. We were moving to Sweden.

CHAPTER SIX

2013-2019

"I used to live in a room full of mirrors; all I could see was me. I take my spirit and I crash my mirrors, now the whole world is here for me to see."

—Jimi Hendrix, "Room Full of Mirrors"

In August 2015, we settled into our new apartment in Gothenburg. My son began school and luckily, on his very first day, he made a new friend—and the rest was relatively easy. I was able to get him a tryout for a top-notch football club, and even though he understood no Swedish at the time, he trained with them three times a week and played matches and tournaments on the weekends. The coaches were outstanding and translated for him for the first three months. After that, Karim, the head coach, insisted that my son was understanding most of his instruction and informed me he would speak Swedish with him from then on. Other than the fact that this club had no bubble (covered turf) to train on during the winter and played outside during even the coldest of days (-14C and snowfall is one day I'll never forget), my son was happy and definitely being challenged and improving. I'd been a full-time soccer mom back in Canada, too; the only difference here was I had no car to escape the rain or cold. Instead, I stood in the face-freezing air, pacing the hazardous ground and sipping lukewarm chai tea. I invested in an ankle-length down jacket and artic durable boots, and still every night after his practices, I was in a hot bath thawing my bones back to life.

I began freelancing here and there and focused the rest of my time on writing feature films and TV series. I applied for funding and was rejected. But I kept writing and I kept applying. I began to make new work connections and realised very quickly that everyone was clinging to their jobs in a sort of angst-filled frenzy. The fear of losing their jobs was tangible. Everyone forty and above was looking over their shoulders for a thief. I understood quickly that I would have to create my own opportunities. I kept carving out TV concepts and writing scripts.

Enter Esther

In the autumn of 2015, I had coffee with a woman I'd known from my early days of directing in Sweden. I hadn't seen her in years, but we immediately got on, and she, too, was on her own path of self-discovery. She enthusiastically recounted her experiences of a woman she'd found online called "Esther Hicks." She told me that this woman channeled a universal entity called Abraham and delivered messages about the Law of Attraction, amongst other things. As my friend eagerly shared her life-changing experiences, my awareness kept turning a neon light on the words Law of Attraction. I'd never heard of Esther Hicks before and was curious as to why my awareness was suddenly so on fire.

I went home that evening and absorbed hours of Esther Hicks. I devoured her messages by the handful like colourful gummy bears. One concept resonated with me so deeply: the idea of alignment or misalignment with your Soul/inner being. The terminology marinated the spongy apparatus of my brain, and my previous ideas screamed a happy, *At last!* It was the same thing I'd termed being *in the zone, attuned,* or *non-resonant,* but her terminology conveyed the concept better, and it was easier to understand.

From that moment on, I began to use Esther Hick's terminology—aligned and misaligned. As I combed through my life experiences, I quickly identified where there had been alignment with my inner being or misalignment. I then began to see how this was connected to the Ego.

The Ego

The Ego serves as an important part of our humanness and gives us identity as a singular being. Ego serves to provide us with opportunities to experience contrast, which, in turn, provides us with some of the most important life lessons. It does this by showing us what we don't want. It is the "fundamental law of life," as the Swiss doctor who founded analytical psychology, Carl Jung, put it, and allows for the conversion "into the opposite." This brought me back to my first conscious thought from childhood, the idea of polarities and contrast—opposite parts of the whole.

The Ego is an abstract feature of our humanness. It is, however, an inaccurate representation of who we truly are because it does not include our entirety. It begins to form the second you arrive on this Earthly plane and is a never-ending challenge. We search for an acceptable image, one that we believe is valued by the outside world. We create a concept of ourselves based on those external deductions, and it's a very slippery slope between an Ego that is aligned with our Soul-self/ higher consciousness and a misaligned Ego that is married to the limited psychology of the unconscious culture/cultivated ignorance within which we live.

What began to reverberate deep within me was this idea of an aligned Ego (a-Ego) and a misaligned Ego (m-Ego). It seemed obvious to me that when you're aligned with your higher consciousness, your Ego automatically joins you. The abstraction of the Ego transforms and transcends with you. I like to think that there are some truly enlightened humans out there who have completely rid themselves of the abstraction of the Ego, but for the rest of us, I'll just assume yours is either aligned or misaligned.

I do not believe the Ego is our enemy. On the contrary, I truly believe the Ego serves to show us exactly what we do want—it's one of our greatest gifts. Like a Gemini twin, your m-Ego is always there, ready to emerge as the hard teacher, but never truly as an enemy. In the words of Alan Watts, "The ego is nothing other than focus of conscious attention."

I wish I could say that once you go from m-Ego country to a-Ego country, you never go back, but unfortunately that's not the case. It works very much like being a tourist. You travel back and forth between the two countries quite freely until one day you decide you want to move to the paradise in which you've been vacationing. You may find that you go back to the *old country* more times than you care to admit, and that's OK. It's like anything—it takes practice. There are no perfect steps to being in alignment, so don't beat yourself up if you suddenly find yourself on the flip side of that coin. The simple fact of being aware that you are misaligned is a gigantic step forward in your shift of awareness.

I'm suggesting that, as part of this human experience and vibrational package, the Ego, like everything else, is either in alignment with our greater consciousness, or not.

I do not think the Ego should be amputated. I see the Ego as a catalyst that leads you closer to *your* inner being, to your alignment and enlightenment, if you're willing to participate. You have an Ego whether you are connected or disconnected, aligned or misaligned, happy or sad. It doesn't disappear when you become enlightened; it just becomes enlightened as well.

I list Wayne Dyer's definitions of *Ego* here, and with great modesty, I presuppose they are in fact definitions of the m-Ego:

> *I am what I have—my car, my house, my possessions.*
>
> *I am what I do—my job, my career, my accomplishments.*
>
> *I am what other people think of me—my reputation, my awards.*
>
> *I am separate from everybody else—I am this body.*
>
> *I am separate from what's missing in my life—I'm not empowered.*
>
> *I am separate from Spirit—I am not Divine.*

In comparison, here is a list of definitions of the a-Ego:

> *I am that I am—I am a spark of Divine Intelligence/Spirit/The Boundless Core of All Consciousness.*
>
> *I am the unfolding of my Higher Self— an expression of The Boundless Core of All Consciousness.*
>
> *I am a reflection of Spirit—I am a spiritual being having a physical experience.*
>
> *I'm one with all that is—I am aligned and connected to The Boundless Core of All Consciousness in all realms of space time.*
>
> *I accept the polarities within me, I have reconciled my shadow—I am empowered.*

As you can see, there is a significant difference between the m-Ego and the a-Ego. For many years, I lived quite happily with my m-Ego, making decisions that seemed adequate and good for me. I know people whose m-Egos lead them to drug addiction, sex addiction, porn, burnout, gambling, fame-seeking, and self-importance, just to name a few.

It's brilliant in design and so very simple. There is no need to defeat your Ego or call it the enemy; you just have to roll with it and allow it to transcend itself. Therein are the greatest life lessons and wisdom. As St. Thomas Aquinas once said, "…it is evil suffering that makes possible the recognition of virtue."

If you allow your m-Ego to direct your life movie, you will have certain experiences. You can either be the B movie director of your life or the A movie director. The choice is yours. You get to decide the genre of the life you're living, the cast of characters who are in it, the wardrobe, the production design, the dialogue, and even the music score. You make directorial decisions about your life movie every single day. Some good, some less so. Decide what movie you want to make, what world you want to live in, and then make every directing decision from that stance.

The movie *The Truman Show* is a great analogy for living a life controlled by the m-Ego. Trapped in a bubble of control, Truman lives a humdrum existence and has to "wake up" first to realise he was ever being controlled. Then, once he is awake and aware of his situation, he must fight his way out by being clever and tricking the m-Ego (the executive producer), who orchestrates every detail of his life.

The executive producer in the film, just like the m-Ego, uses fear to stop Truman from even considering the idea of travel. But the fear is not real; it was all just a ploy to keep him in his naïve bubble of limiting beliefs, in this case, the studio set.

Similarly, if you don't like your life movie, you can't just fire the director or executive producer; you have to wake up first and then begin the conscious process of flipping your script, redirecting the tone until it suits you perfectly. Your life movie is the only movie you'll ever direct and produce where the audience is of no importance. There is no audience. Nobody is watching your movie. It's a selfish piece of work all for, and only ever about, YOU.

Now back to the m-Ego. Anyone who is super-ambitious needs to be wary of the m-Ego. Having the desire to help millions of people is the workings of the m-Ego; *I want to gain one hundred million followers on Facebook, so I can spread my message of positivity.* Yes, even people who claim to be enlightened and want to be of service to humanity struggle to keep the m-Ego in check. *Why?* Because the minute you desire big results is the minute your m-Ego wants to *achieve* something and decides that people are not whole and divine. When the m-Ego decides that people need *fixing,* or that they are *incomplete,* then you're back on that slippery slope of the m-Ego mountain. You can only strive to help yourself in your awakening and then share your experiences with as much humility as possible.

I know a few people who have enormous success and followings and have admitted to this inner tug-of-war. Some then become too commercial and lose sight of the deeper calling and their true meaning of alignment. They start off well intentioned, and then ambition and greed creep into their narrative, and before long, they need to take a step back and self-audit and rewrite. You must do it for you, and only you, with as much humility as possible.

Personal agenda is an aspect of the m-Ego and is really all about not having *any* awareness of what your thoughts are up to. Even the most aware and enlightened individuals can slip off the track. I know I did while writing this book. Every time I slipped, I would remind myself that I was writing this book purely for me, for my growth and expansion. The purpose of putting these words to paper was never to fix anyone else, but rather to create a cathartic process for myself. I was not asked by anyone to write this book. I did it because my inner being invited my hand and thoughts to these pages, and I accepted the proposal. Because in this space of alignment, I felt peacefully connected and integrated with my higher consciousness.

The *real* you is not your m-Ego or any aspects of it. You're an external spark of what I call the Boundless Core of All Consciousness. It's wise not to let your m-Ego inflate itself into the illusion of being God-like. We need to find a balance, balance between learning to control our attitude, effort, and desires, and surrendering to our inner knowing. We must have absolute faith in the natural intelligence of the Universe and our inner wisdom. We must have unshakeable trust. A delicate dance, one that we'll surely rehearse daily for the entirety of our lives.

We all have the ability to transcend this spellbinding, illusory world. We need simply to redirect our hypnotized attention and cultivated ignorance from the external world to the internal one. H. D. Thoreau commented, "The mass of men lead lives of quiet desperation." Let's not be fooled by the hocus-pocus of this make-believe paradise.

Facets of the M-Ego

Here below, we'll look at the main facets of the m-Ego, the ones that most people recognise immediately. The disconnected Ego is the cheater, the liar, the workaholic, the alcoholic, the addict, the abuser, the bully, the overachiever, and a lot of the time, your best friend in disguise. But Ego is only uncomfortable when it's separated from your true essence—when you're misaligned. When you come into alignment with your higher consciousness, when you transcend your ego-centric consciousness, then you feel wonderful, and your Ego is all lit up.

To inspire you to identify if you are in a state of m-Ego, here is a short checklist of negative emotions associated with m-Ego:

- Jealousy (weak negative emotion)
- Envy (weak negative emotion)
- Deceit (weak negative emotion)
- Sadness (mediocre negative emotion)
- Revenge (mediocre negative emotion)
- Frustration (mediocre negative emotion)
- Blame (mediocre negative emotion)
- Self-pity (mediocre negative emotion)
- Defiance (strong negative emotion)
- Anger (very strong negative emotion)
- Cruelty (very strong negative emotion)
- Anxiety (very strong negative emotion)
- Fear (very strong negative emotion)
- Worthlessness (very strong negative emotion)
- Shame (strongest negative emotion)

Another way I detect disconnection from my inner being is to ask myself these questions:

- Am I afraid to speak my truth?
- Do I lack self-worth?
- Do I tolerate toxic people?
- Do I seek external validation?
- Do I seek to please others at the expense of my own well-being?
- Do I engage in negative self-talk?

The stronger the negative emotion, the further down you sink into the misalignment swamp. Journaling became a way for me to process my emotions and identify my m-Ego and reactive tendencies. When I felt like I really needed to vent, I would write a letter to the person I had an issue with and never send it to them. This allowed me to get my feelings of frustration out.

However, be aware as you do this exercise, because the act of venting or ranting can be the same thing as affirming—even on paper. If you're struggling and have to do something with the negative thoughts, write them down, but be sure to release them afterwards. Throw it out, or ceremonially burn it. Let go of the record that's on repeat and play a new song.

When I feel any negative emotions, I redirect my focus of conscious attention and stop the momentum. I become the observer of myself. For me, this was crucial for my growth and is important today in maintaining it.

An easy way I do this is by listing things I'm grateful for, whether it be in my head, out loud, in song, or on a piece of paper.

- I am grateful for my loving son and his excellent health.
- I am grateful for the roof over my head.
- I am grateful for my loving family.
- I am grateful for my excellent health.
- I am grateful for the food in my fridge.
- I am grateful for the money I have that allows me to provide for my family, live well, and give to others.
- I am grateful for my creativity and connection to my inner wisdom.

I keep going until I've generated a bit of gratitude momentum, and then, inspired by Esther Hicks, and Louise Hay, motivational author of several self-help books, I get more specific:

- Things always work out for me. Life is easy for me.
- I am a magnet for abundance and good health.
- Vitality flows into my life and body with ease.

- I am a magnet for love. I am a magnet for creativity.
- I'm looking forward to sharing my gifts with the world.
- I allow my higher consciousness to influence me in positive, creative, and uplifting ways.
- I love knowing that Spirit is ever present to assist me.
- The Universe works *for* me, every day in every moment, always.
- I count. I am important.
- I take in and give out nourishment in perfect balance.
- All is well in my world. I am loved, loving, and lovable. I am worthy, whole, and complete just as I am.

And in no time, I've pulled myself up and out of the marrow of the m-Ego. When I started doing this, I wrote these declarations down on a cue card and had them in my pocket wherever I went. I would pull it out and read from it the minute some creepy m-Ego gremlin raced across my thought-scape. My inner knowing would whisper, *"Run, Forrest, run!"*[3]

Then, after a while, I'd memorized it, and it became a trained response. A reflex. A good habit. I was then able to elaborate and come up with new positive thoughts that would become dominant, joyful intentions. And then it became, *"Easy like Sunday morning."* [4]

When you become awakened to your inner knowing and higher consciousness, you simply do not stand for the old ways; it just doesn't vibe well when you do. Instead you:

- Honour your truth and all of yourself
- Know your worth and the value you bring to the world
- Set boundaries with toxic people
- Feel validated from within
- Inspire others to be themselves

---

[3] From Robert Zemeckis' 1994 film *Forrest Gump*, screenplay by Eric Roth.
[4] From the song "Easy" by Lionel Ritchie, 1977.

- Live unapologetically
- Whisper positive affirmations to yourself all day long

Real transformation always starts with you, the individual. Situations that don't end in your favour do not mean they are bad, but if you stay in a victim mentality, new doors will never open.

It's very difficult to talk to someone about higher consciousness if they're still charmed by the illusion. In my experience, the conversation simply ends with a blank stare and a quick change of subject. Someone once told me never to expect people to believe or even understand what I believe to be true and real. I took that advice to heart and released my expectations of others completely. Everyone is at a unique place of understanding, so there is never any judgment. Translating the language of your Soul is not easy and not of interest to everyone.

Shame

Shame and guilt live in the dark, in your shadow. As you transition from the old undercurrent of control, your awareness of out-of-date patterns slowly begins to awaken. Shame is a painful and complex emotion that can have unconscious effects on our decisions and behaviours. There are many others, but shame is a really difficult one to reach and identify. It's a painful emotion that encompasses the entire self. It holds within it a state of *being* inadequate, unworthy, and dishonourable, and is one emotion that we tend to bury very deeply within. Brené Brown astutely put it this way, "Shame drives two tapes: never good enough and who do you think you are."

Since the core of narcissism is internalized shame, a narcissist will transfer his/her shame onto another, a partner or a child, as a way of self-protecting. This transmission of shame is a real problem and very toxic because it is disguised as something else.

First, one must recognise that shame is present. This may seem obvious, but the majority of people walk around with bricks of shame in their pockets, totally unaware. They have acclimated to the weight of self-loathing and don't even notice it anymore. However, I'll assume that if you've read this far, then you're well aware of the bricks you carry.

I lugged unresolved shame around within me for years, partly because of my early childhood trauma, partly because of my defective relationships, and partly because of my experiences at university. This sliver of shame lay buried beneath my skin for two decades. It convinced and overruled all positive thoughts of self-worth and self-love, and made me believe that I was not honourable. Rewiring your brain to release the shame programming is tough on your own. If you don't have a loving partner, great friend, or therapist, then I suggest you find one.

I designated a friend to be my *buddy*, kind of like an AA sponsor. She was there to hold space for me when I worked through the worst of my trauma. Whether your trauma is shame, anxiety, guilt, or something else, having a supportive person you can call on any time of day is, in and of itself, half the battle. When you know that someone has your back, you're more willing to open up your mind and heart to the awareness of any memory of trauma that arises. With this type of support, you know you are loved and worthy, and therefore, already well on your way to success.

John Makransky shares a meditation practice in *Awakening Through Love: Unveiling Your Deepest Goodness* that can help increase your sense of safety. He believes his "Hand on Heart" meditation and deep breathing activate the parasympathetic nervous system and release oxytocin in the brain. Oxytocin is the hormone of *safety* and *trust*, of *calm* and *connection*. We activate it by feeling loved and cherished. Oxytocin is one the best resources to help people recover from the effects of toxic shame and support a mindfulness practice.

Try his one-minute "Hand on Heart" exercise three to five times a day, and see if it helps you heal your heart and rewire your brain. I highly recommend taking inventory of the people in your life, especially those who support you in an unconditional way. They're the people you want to gravitate towards.

Codependency

Interestingly enough, codependents are perpetually attracted to narcissists, their charm, charisma, apparent confidence, and domineering personalities. It's a mutual tango of passionate dysfunction. The codependent is the pleaser/giver and the narcissist the taker. The narcissist leads and the codependent follows. It seems very easy and natural to them both because they have been playing these roles their entire lives.

The codependent gives up their power and the narcissist thrives on it. Having pirouetted through two of these dysfunctional performances as a codependent, I feel I have some understanding of the dynamics. I finally decided to get some help after my last codependent production ended in divorce.

> I set out on a narrow way many years ago
> Hoping I would find true love along the broken road
> But I got lost a time or two
> Wiped my brow and kept pushing through

–Rascal Flatts, "Bless the Broken Road"

I had a deep suspicion that there was something a bit wonky with me if I'd allowed myself to give up my power, not once, but twice. I swore I wouldn't have another romantic relationship again until I'd figured out the enigma of my repetitive rotten relationship history. Was it just bad luck, like getting on the F train only to realise, ten stops later, you're actually on the M? Or was it pure chance, like skiing in Ontario—there might be snow, but it's never a guarantee? Or maybe, just maybe, there was some unseen pattern at play, a not-yet-understood magnetic stencil that had been designed unconsciously in my younger years and was dictating this vicious cycle.

Many years of seeking, diligent observation, and talk therapy had brought the whole charade to light. I finally understood my default mode: codependent. I came to understand that my choice in partners was connected to an unconscious need to find someone who was familiar. I had been preparing for this dysfunctional role my entire life through the conditioning and patterning of my upbringing. Relentless like a dog hunting for buried bones, I now desperately wanted to erase this impressed motif.

As I write these words, I can tell you honestly it has taken me the better part of twenty years to heal from the codependent blueprint that continuously led me through the dark labyrinth into my shadow. I learned that it is not about apportioning blame but accepting the responsibility to heal and change.

Now I stand in my entire being and own all of me. I know myself and I accept myself, and I do not seek validation from anyone. I am whole just as I am. When we stop expecting to be understood by others who have very little understanding of themselves, well, my friends, that's when we experience a real sense of freedom. In a place of such alignment, we will not attract these types of relationships anymore because as the Law of Attraction states: *"That which is like unto itself is drawn."*

It's important to note that you can find alignment for you, and only you. You cannot do it for someone else, and no one can love *you* into alignment. People can recommend books, movies, and coaches, and share stories and the like, but everyone has to do the work themselves. There are no cheat sheets or shortcuts.

When you discover autonomy and your ability to come into alignment, you will be at peace. Setting an example of alignment, and inspiring through the clarity of that example, is a great way to fire up others. We all have incredible stories of transformation to share, and I encourage you to share yours so that others may be invigorated by them. I believe one of the greatest ways to serve humanity is to tell your story.

The philosopher Will Durant wrote in his book *The Story of Philosophy*, "We are what we repeatedly do. Excellence, then, is not an act, but a habit." Once you've broken through your unconscious patterns and come to the realization that you were conditioned a certain way, then you have to practice being and staying in alignment. It's a new habit you have to create, like eating healthy foods, or exercising daily, or switching the Wi-Fi off. It's hard! It takes diligent participation, but over time you will become excellent at it, just as Durant claims.

We can all face our darkness (if we choose) and uncover parts of ourselves that were disowned, repressed, and rejected. It is, as far as I can tell, one of the most authentic ways of attaining freedom and enlightenment. When we heal, we finally have the *Aha!* moment of understanding of why we broke in the first place. It's dramatic and profound and nothing short of life altering.

Not everyone will understand your journey, and that's perfectly OK, as long as it makes sense to you. Most of us live in a world where, for the most part, the m-Ego is left unsupervised. We're all doing the best we can with the awareness that we choose to have. Yogi Bhajan said, "Love is a process in which ego is lost and infinity is experienced."

Narcississm

One of the most extreme negative energy states is narcissism. A person suffering from narcissism has a defective conscience. Conscience is our inner knowing of right and wrong, and when it's flawed, the person has a hard time relating emotionally to other people—they lack empathy, compassion, altruism, critical self-reflection, and awareness of higher values, amongst other things. It's a pathological condition and can be devastating, as it will affect one's moral and emotional capacity and limit one's depth of experience.

Narcissists have disjointed Egos. Most live in deeply embedded shame, which causes them to divorce themselves from their true Selves and become misaligned. Some were damaged at a very early age through sexual abuse, neglect, faulty parenting, or lack of nurturing, and were made to feel that they were unworthy of love.

One of my ex-boyfriends was an overt narcissist. Super charming and charismatic on the outside, but eventually his dark side emerged, one that he had been hiding from me and the world. He was a sex addict, porn addict, and drug addict. It was a disconcerting and horrifying truth to discover. Ultimately, it was his own cousin who implored me to leave him.

Interestingly enough, in the drama of me leaving him for the last time, he spilled his deepest, darkest secret all over me like boiling water. His mother had sexually abused him in his younger years. The shame was overwhelming for him, and he could not bear the idea of being alone with himself. I told him to get professional help and that I wished he had opened up to me earlier on in our relationship, but that I could not save him—only he could do that. What I learned many years later was that he spiraled out of control after our break-up and dove head-first into a hurricane of cocaine and prostitutes to fill his feelings of shame and worthlessness.

How we raise our children is of the utmost importance. As parents, we sometimes lose sight of the most essential ingredient required for children to flourish: unconditional love. Love really is the magic ingredient that makes everything rise like yeast in your homemade bread. All children need to know and feel, on every level of their being, is that they are loved, so they can soar to their greatest potential.

While the conditions that create narcissism are most definitely complex, it's a combination of nature and nurture. Some were put on a pedestal when they were young, where they were given love based on their performance, looks, or special talents. Adored, yet ignored. They could never be truly loved for who they were, and that is the cause of their deep insecurity.

However they got there, most narcissists need to have continuous adoration to feel worthy. Their sense of self is so weak and insecure they need constant validation from others. If you do something that may unveil their flaws, they go on the defensive and become aggressive. A lot of narcissists lie, not because they are worried the truth will hurt your feelings, but because the truth might provoke you to make a choice that won't serve *their* interests.

Their next weakness is the terror of running out of narcissistic supply. Their supply is people who admire them, people who validate them. When they find such people, they hold on for dear life and "feed" as often as they can.

All of this is, of course, driven by an unconscious m-Ego. For example, the cheater is an unconscious coward who is tempted to chase the fantasy of what could be, instead of courageously addressing their own self-destructive behaviour. Like I said, it takes some grit and courage to examine your imperfections, unconscious conduct, or what Jung called the "shadow side."

And so, the many expressions of the m-Ego are in fact manifestations of our own shadow, and when our shadow is not recognised, it will continue to act out. Anger, jealousy, greed, and addictive behaviours are all shadow expressions. When we bury our shadow aspects, we are disempowered. We must try to reconcile our shadow and stand in the light we've cast. By valuing yourself, and your growth, and integrating all your polarities, you will come to accept your profound nature and be whole. That's exactly what so many "holy" people have done.

Marion Woodman, a Canadian mythopoetic author and Jungian analyst, once wrote, "An ego which sets itself up against Fate is attempting to usurp the power of the Self; it swings from light to dark, from inflation to depression. Only when her ego is firmly rooted in her own feminine feeling can a woman be released from her compulsive behavior."[5] We must try, woman or man, to receive all of ourselves and integrate all our opposites. That, my fellow seekers, is the golden ticket.

Early Childhood Trauma

Shakespeare wrote in *The Tempest*, "What's past is prologue." What has happened to us merely sets the stage for what's to come: either the unfolding of our magnificence, our greatness, our genius, or the repeating cycles of an early unconscious childhood narrative, which for many, involves trauma and the revolving negative emotions of worthlessness and shame.

Up until the age of eight, our thinking mind has not yet developed, so the only way we interpret the world is through feelings—through our unconscious mind. By the time we are fully developed, conscious adults, most of our early childhood memories are buried beneath layers and layers of unconscious and conscious narratives. But these early childhood stories are the very first notes of our life symphony and dictate what tune we'll sing later on.

When I began therapy and started the process of peeling

---

[5] Woodman, *Marion, The Owl Was a Baker's Daughter*, Inner City Books, 1980.

back the many narrative layers I'd spent my life creating, I began to have a reoccurring dream. The setting was an expansive, obscure labyrinth, like a scene out of Tim Burton's *Corpse Bride* with winding staircases endlessly extending every which way. The further down I went, the darker it became. I grew aware in the dream that at the end of each staircase was a room, and inside the room was a child: me. The further down I went, the younger I became. I travelled in this dreamscape on and off for many years, freeing the children that were trapped in the rooms. I would embrace the child I found and wrap her in as much unconditional love as possible, and then bring her up to the surface, to the light, to freedom. Interestingly enough, the inner children I found were always very young. It was obvious that my trapped unconscious trauma was from my very early years of life.

Our early childhood memories are like flies stuck on sticky tape. How do we release them? Well, therapy and inner child work peels back a certain number of layers, but I found that, in my particular case, it was not enough. Those very early, very unconscious memories were bound with super glue.

I came to understand that I could talk till the cows came home but that wasn't going to be enough. I was going to have to rewrite my early childhood narrative. When I became conscious of this idea, a few interesting things began to happen. My biological mother began to visit me in Spirit. She began to share with me happy memories of us together from my childhood. It wasn't all doom and gloom. She showed me how much she loved me. She showed me memories of her feeding me as a baby. She shared moments of her watching me twirl in an open field during a glorious summer day at the cottage. We giggled together, and with a feather, she tickled my arms and face until I couldn't take it anymore. Like a movie projection, she shared these heartfelt early memories with me in the theatre of my mind. I consumed them gleefully, engrossed and bathed in the unconditional love. We had many entertaining, heart-connected moments together, and, one by one, she brought them forward to my conscious awareness.

What followed was a shift. It was a shift in how I perceived myself. I no longer felt the need to hide. I had had a lifelong desire to conceal myself and withdraw, which seemed to be deeply correlated with the negative emotion of shame. However, now, all of a sudden, I felt a real urgency to share myself with the world. And it felt great. It was truly liberating. I understood that I was worthy, and that my uniqueness was my greatest gift. As I shared my heart and authentic self with the world around me, my shame began to melt away. I understood that, up until that point, I'd been putting petrol into an electric car. No wonder I puttered along as I did.

Virtual Reality

I read an article not long thereafter about VRET therapy, Virtual Reality Exposure Therapy, which is a behavioural treatment for PTSD. This therapy targets behaviours that people engage in (most often avoidance) in response to thoughts or memories that are anxiety-filled or angst-provoking. What my biological mother had done in Spirit was a spiritual version of VRET. The goal of VRET is to help reduce a person's fear and to ultimately eliminate the avoidance behaviour. What I began to piece together was that, if we could create computer-generated scenes, people could either confront their feared situations, or experience new loving ones, and in so doing, rewrite their unconscious narratives.

Filmmaker Alejandro Iñárritu created a VR installation called "*Carne y Arena (Flesh and Sand)*," which recreates the experience of crossing the US border from Mexico. I've not had the pleasure of experiencing this installation personally, but I have a friend who did. She recounted the terror she felt and how, towards the end, she literally fell to her knees when Border Patrol officers ordered her to at gunpoint. This made me realise that the realness of VR is very powerful. If it can do that, then can it also heal our deepest traumas and maybe even teach the most hardened narcissist compassion? *Why not?* I don't think this is a theoretical idea anymore; it's been proven to be successful, and the quality of VR is getting better and better every year.

How do we rewrite our early childhood narratives—specifically the ones that were traumatic? I feel that traditional talk therapy helps peel back the first layers of undesirable happenings, and then we need something more potent. We need techniques, such as hypnosis and past life regression, to help us access our deeply buried traumas and allow us to shift core patterns. Then, once we've identified them, we can begin to heal by releasing them or rewriting them. We need to embrace new discoveries like VRET, and think about harmonizing the brain and heart and seriously consider the idea that we are powerful beings with the ability to heal and self-regulate.

I'm open to all techniques and believe that everyone should follow what feels right for them. What works for me may not be the best option for you. But in a general way, I think we can all agree that the steps to rewriting early childhood traumatic incidents look something like this:

- Recall the traumatic event in a safe setting.
- Allow yourself to feel the event.
- Name the emotions that arise and do not judge them.
- Move through the feelings and allow them to dissipate/dissolve (and repeat if necessary). I refer to this as The Burn.
- Get away from anyone who creates trauma in your life.

- Try alternative methods of rewriting your childhood using visualization techniques, hypnosis, VR, EMDR, heart brain harmonization, or other methods.
- Share your stories and experiences with others.

Healing from early childhood trauma is not easy; it's insanely hard, in fact. But it can be done. If you're a parent now raising children, be mindful of how you guide and cultivate these precious and impressionable young beings.

Presence of Mind

I define *presence of mind* as the ability to notice oneself and one's thoughts. As leaders, teachers, and parents, it might be worthwhile to tune into our own calling and presence of mind and be open to helping others feel and hear *their* own inner stirring. Otherwise, we perpetuate an already dysfunctional system that only creates more unconscious thinkers and narcissists. It's a constant tug-of-war between conscious and unconscious mind-sets, between survival constructs and thriving ones.

As a society, and as individuals, we really need to think about ways to allow all children of all ages to thrive and fully express themselves at a mind, body, Soul, and heart level.

We're all constantly unfolding into our own humanity and spirituality. But we must have presence of mind; these are two quite separate things. You can be an enlightened human without being spiritual, and a spiritual being while lacking humanity. Reaching enlightenment in one area does not mean you automatically achieve it in the other. For example, Ösel Tendzin[6] was deemed an incredible spiritual teacher and yet he was a sexual predator who exploited both men and women

---

[6] I've never met him or participated in any of his teachings.

who followed his every word. He may have been spiritually enlightened to some degree, but lacked humanity.

And then there are those who have no spiritual leaning whatsoever but have incredible humanity. One of my dearest friends is such a person. She has dedicated her life to working for large organisations like Save the Children and the International Rescue Committee to help people all around the world attain a healthy, safe, and wholesome life. She doesn't have a spiritual bone in her body and always finds such topics of conversation a little uncomfortable, but her humanity is very well developed indeed.

From my place of understanding, it would seem that we develop our humanity and our spirituality in separate lanes. For some people, those lanes intersect; for others, they do not. I personally believe that my spiritual growth has had a positive impact on my humanity. I can see how I am much less reactive to outside triggers now than I was before my spiritual lane lit up. My son teases me because I never get mad or raise my voice. I smile inwardly because I know it's my spiritual lane infusing my humanity with positive influence.

However, there are many people in positions of power or authority— politicians, law enforcement officers, pastors, spiritual leaders, lawyers, teachers, parents/guardians, pop stars, film execs, doctors, and on and on the list goes—who have failed to keep their m-Ego in check and have succumbed to the seduction it offers, and who, in turn, drag their humanity through the dirt. I'm suggesting that possibly reaching alignment and having a heightened sense of humanity might be more important than spiritual experiences and enlightenment. From what I can tell, being a spiritual teacher who has reached a certain degree of insight may be worth diddly if he or she has not reached alignment with their Soul-self or tuned into their own positive humanity.

There is no one, prescribed way to have presence of mind.

Don't feel pressured to meditate every morning just because Guru X does it and declares it the only way. You don't have to wake up at 5:00 a.m. to join the high achievers' club. Do it if it works for you, but if you don't, it does not mean you cannot grow and expand. Be cognizant of the commercial trappings and expensive workshops of self-proclaimed spiritual teachers and personal-development gurus. Some of these pop stars of spirituality may have started out with great intentions, but unfortunately, many have fallen from grace and into marketing madness. They're programmed to death and claim to have *five easy steps* to make you an enlightened person. Your inbox will be inundated with package deals just for you (you *are* special, after all) and programmes to show you how you, too, can harness your inner power.

If anything, I hope my words have inspired a few to think for themselves and maybe ponder their unconscious record that is on repeat. I'm not promising results, and I don't proclaim to be a guru of any sort. I am, however, sharing my experiences because I believe connecting with the human spirit is one of the most important things we can do.

Find methods that work for *you* and *your* lifestyle.

I imagine *spiritual pickings* much like being in an apple orchard. You pick and choose from all the wise trees until you have a basket full of apples perfectly suited to you. Then, what you do with those apples is up to you. You can eat them at 5:00 a.m. or maybe 8:00 a.m., if that's better for you. You can bake them into pies or make applesauce, eat them raw, or play catch with them. Do whatever you want with the apples of advice you pick, and apply them to your life in ways that work for you. We have too many things to do as it is; we don't need to add more stress or anxiety into our lives. Be flexible with yourself and try not to force anything. Subscribe to a practice that works for you, and that may very well be a completely new one that no one else has come up with yet!

Wake Up

My son has always been pretty level-headed and is by nature cautious and observant. He's played competitive football (soccer) since he was six and has a good understanding that smoking, drinking, and doing drugs don't benefit him or his game. When he was thirteen, I had no reason to believe that he was doing anything remotely clandestine.

One night, while in a deep slumber, I was abruptly ripped out of my dreamscape by a voice that yelled, *"They're vaping!"* I looked around my dusk-filled room, startled. I questioned the validity of the statement immediately. *Vaping? Really?* I went and sat next to my son's bed and watched him in all his dreamy repose. I supposed anything was possible, and he did have a friend or two who lacked confidence and felt the need to gain cool points by doing uncool things. *But was my son vaping?* The clarity of the words came back—*They're vaping*—and so I assumed it was not just him but his entire group of friends. My mind raced with a million different ways of handling the situation.

That day, I called one of the moms who was generally well informed as to our boys' activities. She had a daughter in grade ten who pretty much knew everyone and was well acquainted with the sketchy activity going on at the school. I asked her in a general way if she had heard about our boys vaping. She confirmed it matter-of-factly, "Yeah, it's been going on for a few weeks now. But our boys aren't doing it, they're the only two who didn't try it." I was shocked that my son's friends were vaping at all, but I must admit, I was more amazed by the accuracy of the message I had received the night before.

That day after school, I had a long talk with my son and he, too, confirmed that several of the boys had tried it, and that one boy in particular was doing it rather regularly. He refused to give me names—he didn't want to rat on his friends

(I found his loyalty somewhat endearing) but I already knew who-was-who in this game of smoke and mirrors. I had one more question. Did he know which ninth-grader had sold his friend the JUUL? My son replied without thinking, "Ninth-grader? No, he's in eighth grade." He wouldn't give me a name, but after a little digging, I figured out who the dealer was. I forwarded the information to the school, and within a few days the vaping ring had been dismantled.

I'm not sure I ever would have known about this had I not been woken up so unexpectedly that night. Vaping was just not something I even remotely considered my son's friends would be doing…yet. I thought I had at least one more year of innocence. One thing was for sure, my inner voice (or that of one of my Spirit guides) was active and coming through loud and clear.

Conditioning

I'm no expert on the topic of parenting, nor am I a psychologist, psychiatrist, or medical professional. I'm just a parent trying to figure it out—observing and learning as I go.

From my perspective, it seems that our parents, our culture, our schools, our religions, and society at large *condition* and *train* us to comply. They want us to live in a box and think in a box. They don't like it when we sing too loudly or speak our truth too honestly. John F. Kennedy once said, "Conformity is the jailer of freedom and the enemy of growth." I believe this to be true; yielding to the desires of others, to the misleading concepts and cultivated ignorance they try to sell you, is a straight path to disconnection with your Higher Self. If you're going to fail, at least fail on your own terms. And just for the record, I've failed a gazillion times.

The seat of so much unhappiness, depression, suicide, divorce, food disorders, and mental illness seems to be rooted in misalignment with our higher consciousness. It's like a never-ending game of dominoes where everyone goes down and passes it around. Unless you can somehow rise above the game board and see the tiles for what they are, you, too, will pass it on. Simply put, most peoples' biases and conditioning are like the numbers on a domino tile—you match or project your number onto the next tile, your offspring, and on and on it goes.

Our conditioning is like an anchor that ties us to our beliefs. It's forced expectation, and in most cases, does not make the individual happy, because they are just that, an individual. A unique energetic expression wanting nothing more than to express him- or herself in a singular, purposeful way.

> *Well, now if I were president of this land*
> *You know, I'd declare total war on the*
> *pusher man.*

—Steppenwolf, "The Pusher"

For the better part of my life, that's exactly what I did. The box of conformity that was being presented to me, and everyone who was pushing its ideals and values, got a taste of my refusal to cooperate and conform. One thing I didn't do: "I never touched nothing that my spirit could kill." I was a rebel, and my cause: personal freedom.

Tug-of-War

These external conditions become self-imposed biases that we as individuals pick up from our families and unconscious culture, which we then claim as our own. This, in turn, creates a kind of magnetic push and pull between true Self and m-Ego self. The eternal tug-of-war between barking Ego and whispering Soul. These biases are anything but our truth. They are so far from our true nature that it's really hard to find our way back to self-love, true Self, and alignment. We get lost in the maze of our m-Ego, and, quite frankly, it's an exhausting journey of *unbecoming* and *unlearning* to find one's way back to the awareness of inseparability—an undertaking that requires copious amounts of stamina and relentless participation.

Parents are just people who had kids. No one gave them the how-to-raise-conscious-munchkins manual, or forced them to take the prerequisite *Raise Connected Tots 101*, so what the heck do they know about raising kids? Nothing. Nada. Zip all. They just do what was done unto them. You can see already what's wrong with this picture. The most difficult and important job on the planet, and everyone is allowed to just wing it. No one checking in on your progress, no supervision, no corrections to what might be poorly done.

I don't claim to have all the answers to childrearing, but I do suggest taking a deeper look at yourself before you unintentionally pass on all your unconscious behaviours and traits to your mini-magnificents. Dare to look yourself in the mirror, survey your triggers, your psyche, your behaviours, your shadow Self. *What lingers there? Have you taken your garbage out?*

Raising kids is like building a rocket ship and launching it into space. You create this incredible vessel, a miracle, really, who needs expensive insurance coverage, lots of special attention to detail, constant care and supervision, and is tested over and over before blastoff. T minus eighteen years to adulthood launch, this little rocket needs solid ground support, mega amounts of fuel for flight, and a skilled launch director or two to get the intricate apparatus ready for liftoff.

Do parents work on themselves before having kids? Do they dig deep to understand themselves and transcend their own shadow? Are they even aware of the shadow and all that it controls? The answer is sure, some parents have done the work and are consciously parenting, but unfortunately, the vast majority are not. And nobody—especially not I—can tell you, or anyone else for that matter, not to have children. The world keeps spinning, and an average of 360,000 babies are born every day on this planet. *So what happens?* If you're a child that is trusting and empathetic, then you expect other people to be that way, too, especially your parents. They're supposed to love you unconditionally, after all!

Well, when the unconscious parent has a disconnected Ego, the parent will treat their child(ren) in ways that seem completely unacceptable to the unsuspecting child. The parent may gaslight their child, belittle, neglect, deceive, ignore, rage at, and, at worst, physically or sexually abuse them. What is so painful for children is that they don't understand why their parent(s) are doing this. It makes no sense to them.

I think it's fair to suggest that if you don't want your life to be interrupted, then you may want to opt out of having children. But if you choose to have a *bambino*, then be prepared to *possibly* be awoken to your blind spots, those areas of yourself brought forth from shadow that you've never had the pleasure of meeting before. Yeah. Fun stuff. However, if you become aware and even embrace your shadow, there is opportunity for real personal growth and wisdom.

I have definitely not mastered the art of raising kids, but I try to expand my know-how by reading books, seeking counsel, asking questions, being in alignment, and listening to and sharing stories with other parents. It's not perfect, but at least it's an attempt to try and improve my already weak skill set. Here is a list of a few of my favourite books on the subject of consciously raising kids, and raising conscious kids:

- *The Conscious Parent* by Shefali Tsabary, PhD
- *The Awakened Family* by Shefali Tsabary, PhD
- *The Art of Screen Time* by Anya Kamenetz

- *What Do You Really Want for Your Children?* by Dr. Wayne W. Dyer
- *Blend* by Mashonda Tifrere

They say it takes a village; sure, but who are the villagers? *Are they operating out of alignment or misalignment? Are they conscious players or unconscious-culture shareholders?* As people become aware of their own crappy upbringing, one hopes they will become conscious enough to try new ways of parenting instead of slipping into their parents' dysfunctional shoes. I read somewhere, "If you don't heal from what hurt you, you'll bleed on the people that didn't cut you." Unfortunately, the catch-22 is that it's only when you wake up that you realise the repeating patterns at play.

I believe that it must be easier to build strong, conscious, emotionally intelligent children from the beginning, rather than to repair misaligned, broken adults. Because, let's be honest, most adults quit trying to shatter their walls of imposed belief after only a few attempts. The fortress they spent years building for survival and protection is so thick it's almost impenetrable. This is because survival programming is stronger than thriving mechanisms, and it's an exhausting endeavour to shift gears. It demands a lot of inner strength—a warrior spirit and a willingness to look in the mirror and own your BS.

Fortunately, today, there is an ever-growing community of people who are trying new methods of parenting and educating. People who are aware that the old ways may not be conducive to raising emotionally intelligent and aligned children. It's beneficial to the global collective to have children who grow up to serve and give back to their communities, children who go on to thrive and have fulfilling partnerships, children who grow up and participate in the world in purposeful ways.

There are many leading-edge schools, and new schools of thought, that are implementing alternative strategies and programmes that allow children and adults to thrive in their uniqueness and expand in areas not available in traditional schooling systems. Mindvalley is one that comes to mind. I have yet to participate in any of their courses (not for lack of desire) but highly recommend you browse their site; it might be a good fit for you, or for someone you know. The founder and CEO, Vishen Lakhiani, is passionate about enabling people to reach their true potential.

I also believe in consciousness-based education and have started to meditate with my son. He connects very easily with his higher consciousness, and every once and a while, he'll bounce into the room with Tigger enthusiasm and declare, "Let's meditate!" I believe this has helped him find his centre, especially during emotionally challenging times. Our current education does not promote inner knowing at all.

The headmaster of the high school I went to in France was very disconnected. Somewhere on her journey, she had learned that discouragement was an effective tool to get students to work harder to achieve better grades. It was never about what a student wanted; it was always about how a student performed on a scale of one to seven. However, thanks to her and those horrid *conseil de classe* sessions, my inner wild woman was awakened.

Unfortunately, over time, I began to believe what all the hypnotized fools were saying. I began to doubt myself and my inner calling. Slowly, my wild woman was being tamed by my m-Ego. Not being able to identify or even see the enemy, she retreated and lay down for a very, very long nap.

It doesn't matter how mighty we are; if we've been beaten down over and over, if we've been told enough times that we are worthless and pathetic, if people have broken our trust time after time, if we've been manipulated and abused, extorted and double-crossed, if our heart has been stabbed by adultery and dishonesty, if our spirit has been shattered by wicked words, well then it's hard to stay in our lane of alignment and hold our truth torch high. It's damn next to impossible, because we begin to believe all that falsity.

The trauma we've experienced has cut us down to nothing but a stump of a human. We curl up our mighty tail and shut down our belly of fire. Yesterday's vigour and passion are now just a negligible glow of ash. We're completely disconnected. We lost the tug-of-war. We hide and are never found. That is what trauma leaves behind. Yet, we always have a choice to get back up. Always.

The analogy I received in a meditation once went something like this: *People in your life have sucked the elixir out of you and then spat it out into a baggie. They then callously threw it into the freezer and forgot about it. Then, many moons later, in a desperate search for ice cubes, they found the baggie buried deep beneath the frozen meats. They smashed it with a hammer into a thousand pieces that sparkled like diamonds and dumped it into their liquor. They served it up in a big-ass glass of Scotch and drank it, completely unappreciative of what they were swallowing.* This analogy struck a very deep resonance within me, and my inner knowing followed it with these words: *You allowed it. You will grow from it.* And in that moment, I took ownership for everything good or bad that had ever happened to me.

Just because you're down in the mud, doesn't mean you can't stand up and start another game of tug-of-war. You see, the people that seem to be your enemies are playing a very important role in the intimate tango of virtue and vice. These dance partners are parading their wicked behaviours all over the stage for you to witness, which in turn inspires you to seek answers and clarity. I learned so much about myself from those contrasting chaotic relationships, which ultimately led me on this curious road of self-discovery.

So, my warrior friends and truth seekers alike, I ask you to dig deep if you're feeling like you just can't fight anymore. Find the flame within, no matter how weak the glimmer, and get up on your feet and continue on. Do not relent. You are powerful. You can and you will win this battle.

It all comes back to polarities. *How do we know action if there is no inaction? How do we know difficulty if there is no ease? How was I to know clarity if there was no chaos?* We don't take it for granted when we come from an experience of polarity. Instead, there is a great sense of relief and acknowledgment of how much better it feels to be in a place of love and clarity than chaos and confusion. And ultimately, when we are able to remain in the centre of these contrasting pillars, that's when we're able to move consciously in any direction.

I believe there are two truths to be found in the pause between polarities; the truth of nothingness or the truth of boundless creative consciousness. I personally have found the latter. It reminds me of Robert Frost's poem *The Secret Sits:*

> We dance round in a ring and suppose,
> But the Secret sits in the middle and knows

PART III

THE MAGNIFICENT
MAPLE

CHAPTER SEVEN

Shifts & Letting Go

"All I can be is me—whoever that is."

—Bob Dylan, *In-Beat*
Magazine, May 1965

The second shift in my awareness came after I fell into a depression following a miscarriage. I already described this in Chapter Three, so I won't go into great detail here, but the heavenly visitation that dropped in on me that morning, the glorious apricot-lemon–coloured vision was what prompted my second momentous shift. It alone was not enough to completely move me from operating out of a disconnected Self. What it did do was get me out of aspects of my m-Ego, specifically sadness and despair. The vision literally shifted my vibration from one of depression to one of hope.

I view hope as a derivative of love—an optimistic lifeline in this human experience. It's also a very powerful tool in the process of transformation, as it allows us to cherish an expected outcome with positivity.

As my emotional well-being shifted gears, it quite literally kicked my depressed butt out of bed and got me to quit smoking within ten days. The vision of the unbounded being was so powerful that I went from being an atheist to suddenly knowing beyond a shadow of a doubt that a higher power existed—all in a matter of about thirty seconds. That extremely brief period of time changed the course of my entire life. I used to be one to giggle at the hippies who spoke of free love, and snootily strut past the self-help section in bookstores. I always raised a curious eyebrow when people spoke of far-out things like Souls and reincarnation. But the rapture and love of this unqualified vision gave me immediate faith.

What I know now, which I didn't know then, was that this vision marked the second phase in my spiritual journey of self-discovery. This new awareness and consciousness, one that enlightened me to the *fact* that I am not operating alone in the Universe, was a huge step in my understanding that there was more to life than what was currently being served on the dinner menu. *Was there another menu, another restaurant entirely?* Things were not as they seemed to be, and I was spiritually hungry to find out more.

One night, I had a dream that illustrated in a concise way the resistance I'd been putting up for so many years. I was standing in the middle of a road, holding an umbrella, not over my head, but in front of my chest. I was using it as a shield against a gang of thugs. What the dream illustrated was that the things coming at me in life were not dangerous or life threatening. They were *opportunities* and *possibilities*—glorious *potentials* that I had only to say yes or no to. However, I was standing there fighting *all* of them off with my umbrella of might, as if these potentials were daggers of death. I was *resisting* all of them. I'd been trained to live in survival programming, victimhood mode, and to protect myself at all costs.

My early childhood experiences had taught me that the world was unsafe and fraught with danger at almost every turn. In my dream, my umbrella was swept away by a mighty gust. I stood unarmed and vulnerable. *Now what?* An empty, white swivel chair suddenly appeared in the middle of a dark intersection. A stark white light illuminated the chair from above. *Sit.* I woke up abruptly with the prevailing idea that there was a different narrative to partake in. Slowly, I began to implement this idea of *nonresistance* and *surrender* into my daily life. I found many wonderful videos by Esther Hicks on this specific topic. And so, I consciously began a daily commitment of checking my reactive stance at the door.

Every time something came up that made me put up my umbrellas of defense, I stopped myself and parked that protective attitude at the door. *So what if I get wet?* I surrendered to the possibility first, and then made a choice. Instead of writing it off or fighting it off before I even knew what *it* was, I *allowed* it to enter my sphere, and then I *surrendered* to it, and either *accepted it*, or *let it go*. Choices, my friends—we all have license to choose, but if we fight off the offerings before we even know what they are, we literally make no progress. Put your metaphorical umbrellas of defense down and see what shows up. You'll be amazed and delighted, mark my words.

Sometimes we get struck by lightning, figuratively speaking, or have a vision, like I did; we get inspired by a book, roused by a conversation with a friend, or hear a song that triggers a stirring within us. In "The Dream of Life," Alan Watts eloquently sums up what happens when you undergo a shift in awareness and begin to awaken to the illusory reality of this world:

> *If you awaken from this illusion and you understand that black implies white, self implies other, life implies death (or shall we say death implies life?) you can feel yourself not as a stranger in the world, not as something here unprobational, not as something that has arrived here by fluke—but you can begin to feel your own existence as absolutely fundamental.*

The Soul

The concept of the Soul became a simple knowing for me. I was drawn to Hinduism and felt a real kinship with the tenet of reincarnation. Our Soul returns to this physical realm of duality in a new body and repeats this over and over as often as it likes. I woke up one morning from a vivid dream with this poem floating in my awareness:

> In a dream it became so clear
> The body—an overcoat for the Soul
>
> I leapt outside myself on
> The last exhale of death
>
> Upon which I knew I could re-enter
> On the wings of just one breath
>
> I gazed upon my body—happy and free,
> Tickled that my mind and thoughts were still with me
>
> Death of body is not death of Soul. She dances and sings
> Through centuries of love, learning, and woes
>
> Ever curious, always free. I am
> My Soul, and my Soul is always me

> *Gothenburg 2016*

This poem took me back to my out-of-body experience, and I immediately understood that what I had done that day was to release my Soul through deep belly breathing. All my faculties of consciousness remained with me as I travelled through infinite dimensional space, and when I was ready, my Soul reentered my body through breath once again.

I was waking up to the true nature of our world; the veils of ignorance were lifting. I began to suddenly not give a damn about the expectations of what seemed to be a declining and dying culture. It's a truly flawed premise in which people seek validation from others instead of thriving in their alignment and connectedness with their own higher being. We were brought up to have a very selective consciousness, to have conditioned responses, which in turn means you have a selective world based on that consciousness. My world had suddenly opened up to new octaves on the consciousness scale, and it was showing me new perspectives.

I agree that it's hard to understand, let alone believe, any of this if you have not experienced it yourself, but I believe we can all shift and transcend the hypnosis. If you seek to wake up, you will inevitably have some form of shift in perception that will lead you to experience a new point of perspective. I believe the desire alone to know, to seek, to move from transactional to transcendental, is more than enough to bring this revamping about. How that will happen will be different for everyone.

Surrender

By 2016, I had participated in a myriad of experiences, ones that had brought me joy, unconditional love, loss, betrayal, anxiety—a whole spectrum of emotions. I took the time to review my life. I wanted to see at what points in my life something had happened by what appeared to be pure *randomness* and *lack of resistance*, and when things had worked out because I'd forced the yield, so to speak. What I realised rather quickly was that the times in my life when I was aligned with my higher consciousness, things simply flowed and gelled and there was a real sense of ease to everything. When I was misaligned, things were difficult and onerous, accompanied by a feeling of trying to *force* things into being. It became clear that the trick was to relinquish the illusion of control and hand over the controls to my higher knowing. Trying to control anything at all is an absurd waste of time.

Being in charge does not mean you are in control. It would appear that the Higher Self is in control. However, the misaligned Ego thinks it's in control and is sure it knows what's best for you. This is why letting go of the pretext of being in control is so important. When the Ego becomes a part of your aligned team, it works with you and puts up no resistance. It doesn't disappear; it just becomes your ally. It's quite simple, and yet very difficult to identify at first glance; the Ego is fighting because we are putting up resistance. *Why are we resisting?* Because we are not accepting. *Why are we not accepting?* Because we want to be in control. *Why do we want to be in control?* Because it gives us the illusion of being in charge of our own destiny. When we stop doing this and hand over the reins to our inner knowing, we allow our true nature to pull us in the right direction. We begin the process of co-creating with our Higher Self. And the perk: You feel ecstatic like a kid on Christmas morning.

But when we try and control things or *force the yield*, as it were, it very rarely works out. In 2018, I found myself trying to do exactly that. The more I tried to get funding for my TV series, the more rejections I received. I finally stopped and surrendered to my inner being with an exhausted, *If it's meant to happen, then I'm sure you'll take care of it.* I had invested approximately four years of my life writing, rewriting, pitching, and selling this series, to no avail. I finally shelved it and decided to listen to my inner GPS, which was nudging my creative juices towards the writing of this book.

And just like that, when I let it go, a producer unexpectedly took interest in my TV series. We signed a six-month shopping agreement. At the end of the six months, a few local networks had passed on it, and my producer flew out to LA to present it to Netflix. At this point, I decided it was time to look for an agent. In the end, we received a *no thanks* from Netflix, but I now had two agents offering me representation.

The one sure way to become one with everything is to trust your higher guidance completely. I cannot predict what will happen next in my life story, but I know that when I act out of complete surrender to the coaxing of the bigger *all-knowing-me*, things tend to be easy and effortless. Don't get me wrong. Writing a book takes effort and discipline; yet it's done with such joy and pleasure when it's in alignment with your higher consciousness that it's not work, but rather a labor of love. A debt of honour. An act of grace.

So be wary of trying to delegate authority; the more you let go and trust your connection with your inner being, the more you'll realise so many of your anxieties and desires to achieve and control are based on your *not* knowing you're a spark of the divine. Or as the Hindus say, "We are all God in disguise."

Emotional & Spiritual Progress

Resisting alignment and playing hide-and-seek with your true Self is utterly exhausting—I know because I did it for decades! The effort required to keep the m-Ego going and to fight your genuine nature is a nonsensical misuse of energy. That was me, in a nutshell, for far too many years.

I had a very unsettling experience once that shoved my m-Ego straight into my awareness, where I could no longer deny it. My disconnected Ego wanted my ex to suffer the way

I had suffered after his betrayal and abandonment. My m-Ego said, *Now it's his turn to know what that feels like.* In all my misalignment, I encouraged my ex to do a DNA test to find out whether his second child (my son's brother from another mother) was in fact his biological child. My m-Ego and personal agenda were skipping hand-in-hand together like little kids on Halloween night, elated with anticipation of the sugar rush to come. My m-Ego had me believing that we were about to be vindicated, that these test results would lead to some sort of payback. When the test results came back positive, my m-Ego hobbled into a corner, tail between its legs, utterly ashamed. I was, for the first time, in a kind of emotional void, no longer aligned with my m-Ego, and feeling very raw and uncomfortable as I leaned towards the call of my bigger Self. I remained in a sort of vacuous space for about five days and went through the seven stages of grieving in record time:

1) Desperate—I demanded answers!
2) Denial—How could this be?
3) Bargaining—Maybe the results were wrong?
4) Anger—I didn't get what I wanted and now I was pissed off.
5) Depression—Bugger me, I thought I had it all figured out.
6) Initial acceptance—Well, OK, then, the science is 99.9 percent accurate, after all.
7) Hope—I'm so glad we can now all just get on with life.

In that experience, I quite clearly saw my m-Ego in action. It was an incredible lesson in misalignment. As my m-Ego took its last breath, I experienced all the emotions that go along with a real death. My m-Ego had been my trusted on-and-off BFF for so many years. Now I was finally free to carve out another path, to veer in another direction. A new trajectory towards alignment and love.

However, I don't think anyone ever reaches a perfect place of connection with Spirit because, in the pursuit of perfection, there is no room for growth. Instead, you simply want to stay in your lane of connectedness and continue on that path towards more expansion, towards the continuous unfolding of your Soul.

Let the Horse Lead

Our predicament as human beings is completely mystifying. I don't believe there is one answer; all we can do is allow ourselves to be the recipients of all that is meant for us—to get into the right lane and put down our umbrellas of defense. Our world of relativity and comparative experiences teaches us exactly what we don't want, and, through these polarities, we slowly begin to choose more wisely. We choose to be happy, to have clarity, passion, and joy, and we spin the momentum of our wheel in a fortuitous direction. It's important to understand that no one can love you into alignment; they will only suffer defeat every time. "Your empowered state of alignment is a self-assigned experience, and the way you find it is by feeling into one good thought, one joyful experience, at a time," as Esther Hicks so wisely asserts.

In your alignment with your higher consciousness, with your Ego in a place of positive emotions, you attract positive things to you. In the exact same way as the m-Ego loves the m-Ego—the Law of Attraction does not discriminate—the a-Ego loves the a-Ego. If you are in the lane of love, you will welcome things of a loving vibration. Plain and simple. The key is to let go of the reins that you think are directing your horse and carriage. Let the horse lead the way—he has better instincts and a superior sense of the road that lies ahead. Kick back and let him take you for a ride. Just be ready to jump off and into your next adventure when he comes to a stop.

Joy & Playfulness

As my awareness evolved, it became clear to me that everything, absolutely everything, is vibrational energy. A lot of what keeps us out of the resonance of joy are underlying negative emotions and thoughts. This negativity can lie dormant for years, if not your entire life, like my forgotten sliver of shame. But we must remember, a negative mind will never create a positive life, and it's important to be playful and include joy in our lives daily.

Our minds and bodies have the innate wisdom required to overcome our shadow side, and seeking professional guidance or assistance can be tremendously helpful during this process. It's called healing, or shadow work, and the process reveals parts of us that were disowned, repressed, or rejected. I believe this is the work of awakening.

When a person is out of alignment with the love and resonance of their inner being, they act and vibrate in a lower frequency—one of negative emotion. They fly their plane at a very low emotional altitude and threaten to crash and burn. However, our inner being is always offering us a vibration of love and adoration. We can choose to resist it, which causes pain and suffering, or we can choose to align with it, and be free and at ease. If nothing else works for you, then simply change the subject altogether and move your conscious attention to a more positive theme or topic. If that doesn't work, then sing, baby, sing. Music and anything that brings you joy nourishes you on an emotional and soul level.

Here is my pick-me-up playlist that immediately pulls me out of my murky misalignment mode:

"Got to Be Real"
    "Got to Be Real" by Cheryl Lynn

"Rise up this morning, smiled with the rising sun…"
    "Three Little Birds" by Bob Marley

"I can see clearly now, the rain has gone…"
    "I Can See Clearly Now" by Johnny Nash

"I believe when I fall in love with you it will be forever…"
    "I Believe (When I Fall in Love)" by Stevie Wonder

"We are family, I got all my sisters with me…"
    "We Are Family" by Nile Rodgers and Bernard Edwards for Sister Sledge

"Well, she was just seventeen…"
    "I Saw Her Standing There" by The Beatles

"This girl is on fire…"
    "Girl on Fire" by Alicia Keys

"I've been watching you for some time…"
    "Ocean Eyes" by Finneas O'Connell

"I can hear the trumpets blowing…"
    "The Update" by Beastie Boys

"Let me stand next to your fire…"
    "Fire" by Jimi Hendrix

"Go, get your freak on…"
  "Get Ur Freak On" by Missy Elliott

"Freedom"
  "Freedom" by Pharrell Williams

Create your own go-to playlist of uplifting songs, and sing whenever you feel yourself slip. Or blast your favourite tunes and dance into delirium—an instant recalibration of lower frequencies.

Decide for yourself what brings you joy, what your idea of a good time is. Don't feel pressured to do what works for others; integrate concepts into your life that work for you. Maybe it's being in the ocean and swimming with mammals, or forest bathing, playing an instrument or doing sports, drawing, building miniature worlds, meditating, or cuddling with your pet. Peace, quiet, or solitude, maybe? Or maybe travelling, writing, cooking, painting, or dancing. *What does your Soul crave to feel alive and well?* Find the things that satiate your Soul-self with delight and make sure to do them at least once a day.

I plan these playful activities into my day with all seriousness. Playing basketball is a definite mood-lifter for me, and doing it with my son brings extra cheer to my Soul. Writing, boxing, swimming, skiing, singing, dancing, alone time, painting, sharing stories, laughing, and cuddling are *my* Soul's must-haves. We need to be mindful that our bodies and minds work best when in pleasant levels of experience. Sometimes, this may seem impossible because we have a job that really isn't all that fun, but it pays the bills. However, we do have time during lunch and after work to prioritize our joy. These activities of jubilance and *aliveness* drown out the broadcast of the m-Ego and the mundane daily grind—they help us to find our way back to our Soul core and connection. A place where we meet our best, happiest, most genius selves. If we don't wake up to who and what we truly are, to what ignites our Soul song, then one day we may wake up completely empty and bankrupt.

It's easy to get entangled in the maze of your m-Ego and be lead astray in the world of unconscious promises. It takes a certain amount of courage to do the work of awakening to who you truly are. So instead of wasting your energy fighting your true nature in what you think is self-defense, drop your guard, and open yourself up to receiving the symphony of your life. Be the needle that co-creates with the vinyl record, and play your song! Thriving is what is meant for us all, and joy is the foundation to growth.

CHAPTER EIGHT

Beyond the Visible

"...we know what we are but know not what we may be."

–William Shakespeare, *Hamlet*

In 2018, I awoke from a strange dream. In the dream, I had done a DNA test and found out I was 100 percent Japanese. I looked in the mirror and furrowed my brow. *Say what?* I didn't look Japanese whatsoever.

All that day I was shadowed by the prevailing idea that I am not who I think I am. I am more than I know. I am in fact divergent from the person I am acting out in this moment. We all have ideas about who and what we are, based on external beliefs and biases, and for the most part, they are false truths. Following this astute dream, I launched myself into the uncharted world of writing this memoir. I was finally ready to share myself in an authentic way. I gave fear the boot and began to emboss the page with my naked truth. I initiated a process of allowance, and my soul began to permeate the page.

As I continued to claim a higher vibrational energy and align more and more with the resonance of my Soul-self, remembrances of past lives began to flood into my awareness. One of the very first ones I had was rather distressing.

In one lifetime, I was a woman who died in childbirth.

I remember the bed had a brass frame and was under a large window facing onto a garden. As I looked down from above, the bed was completely soaked in blood, and people were scurrying around. One woman sat in the corner of the room, trembling and crying. My body was lifeless, and it was obvious I was dead. My belly was round with the expectancy of life, but I could not see or hear a baby. I got the distinct feeling that the baby had not been born.

In a meditation some months later, I witnessed another past life where I was obviously very poor and had gone into labor in the black of night in a cobblestone alley somewhere. The ground was slick with rain and blood. I was all alone and died on the street, trying to give birth.

I asked my higher consciousness for guidance as to why these remembrances were being shown to me. The answer was simple: to help me understand why in this lifetime I had been so reluctant to have children, and moreover why, in this current life, my birthing process was so laborious and difficult.

What I was beginning to understand was that, on a quantum level, we unconsciously carry forward energies from our past lives into our current lives. A vibrational/quantum imprint, if you will, is carried forward in the quantum aspect of our DNA. What I didn't know was how momentous the day of my son's birth in this lifetime truly was. Apart from the obvious miracle, it was the first time in hundreds of years that I had had an incarnation where my human body survived childbirth. It's not common for women to die in childbirth in the Western world these days, but I distinctly remember in this lifetime the hustle in the OR following my C-section as I began to bleed out, the nurse fainting, and that feeling of losing connection with my body. But I survived. This time I did not die.

By giving birth successfully in this life, I had effectively rewritten the imprint of *dying in childbirth*. I changed my energetic coding, and rewrote the potentials for my future lifetimes as well. When we become aware of our past traumas, we can then begin the process of healing them. And healing them means the pain no longer controls our current or future lives. If you believe that everything exists in one colossal "now" moment, then you can begin to understand how our future selves, and the decisions and choices we make now, influence our past, present, and future moments. If you go fishing in the bottomless reservoir of the worldwide web, you will find people doing experiments on this specific topic.

Pain and trauma travel through our lineage, generations, and families until someone is ready to feel it, heal it, and release it. If you heal something in the quantum field, it automatically heals your offspring's quantum field as well, so you're doing the work not just for you, but for your children, too. You share physical DNA as well as quantum aspects with them. So, if you believe, as I do, that you have lived for eons, here and in other worlds and dimensions, you can only imagine how may "relatives" you have out there in the cosmos and in worlds beyond our current awareness. Mending your quantum stencil affects beings you have no current awareness of. Yeah, I know, it's far out for sure.

Max Planck, the father of quantum theory, speculated that consciousness was fundamental, and that matter was derived from it. This means that consciousness is energy on a quantum, subatomic level, and contained in our bodies, but not a part of them. This is what I experienced personally during my out-of-body experience, when I understood that consciousness does not atrophy. Ever. Some scientists wanted to know where this consciousness goes after death and if it comes back. Scientists are beginning to understand and prove that consciousness is not dependent on the physical brain to survive, and that it can integrate into a new brain and share past-life memories with it.

We're on the cusp of leading-edge discoveries just like Louis Pasteur with his research that supported germ theory some two hundred years ago. A few hundred years before that it was believed impossible to cross a huge ocean safely in a vessel, and once upon a time the world was thought to be flat. *Is it really that far-fetched to believe that consciousness is separate from the body and goes on to exist after our death?* I cannot prove this scientifically, but my personal experiences tell me yes, of course this is possible. The Soul *is* consciousness and is ever growing and expanding through lifetimes and other experiences, through cosmic, quantum, and galactic adventures, to heaven only knows where. Our history shows us that the cog of culture makes many revolutions before new truths about reality catch into gear. I believe that the valves of new truths are about to open.

There is a lot of research currently underway at the University of Virginia that deals with this specific theme: The Science of Reincarnation. Some of this research investigates children's claims of past lives. Their current families, sometimes using the internet, and sometimes having the ease and ability to travel, are able to verify details of these lives and confirm their children's stories. This is amazing, considering only fifty years ago these children would have been told their stories were nothing but products of their wild imaginings.

I believe that past life experiences can range from truly traumatic events, such as dying at childbirth, or drowning, or dying in car accidents, to amazingly joyful and loving experiences, like happy relationships, successful careers, and peaceful family lives. When a person is brave enough to allow a past trauma to rise up and burn through their being, they essentially heal it, and release it, leaving a higher vibrational resonance behind. It's not easy, by any means, and I have had the uncomfortable pleasure of healing many traumas in this lifetime.

Raising your awareness increases your energetic vibration, and, in turn, allows for greater DNA efficiency. It allows you to remember things quickly. As I continue to reach for higher vibrational energy, more and more is available to me. Now I choose to have positive past lives brought forth so I can tap into the energy and wisdom of those lifetimes. But every once in a while, an unexpected past life will come into my current awareness, and I'll connect the dots and understand why it was brought forth.

In my brief experience, I've come to understand that consciousness encompasses aspects, and these aspects have different qualities. The number of aspects of consciousness a human chooses to have will vary, but from my perspective, and somewhat limited understanding, it would seem that there are many varying qualities of consciousness, possibly even an infinite number. Think of consciousness like an enormous beach. When you reach your hand into it, you realise it's made up of many tiny granules, and each granule is unique. The beach appears to be one big singular concept, but it is in fact made up of many petite seeds of sand.

Being available to these "seeds" or qualities is like being a receiver to frequencies, because, like all things, aspects of consciousness are vibrational. If you're tuned into the right station, you'll receive them. And so, the basis for human consciousness appears to be made up of the vibrational qualities of awareness, sensitivity, and understanding. I created these terms for my own use, and I add new "seeds" or qualities to the list as they arise in my awareness:

- QR, for Quantum Ribbon, a quality of consciousness that includes the Quantum Ribbons of DNA and the vast storage of all our many lifetimes. With this aspect/quality awakened, we are able to map our Soul's journey, past and future, if we so desire. Some people call this the Akashic Record.

- L, for Lotus, a quality of consciousness that includes the ability to read people's conscious energy, past, present, or future, and encompasses all things, living or dead. Psychics and mediums have this aspect awakened.

- SC, for Soul Collector, a quality of consciousness that appears when we die and collects fragments of our consciousness just before we transition.

- E, for Empathic and ESP, qualities of consciousness that allow the individual to sense and be receptive to the sensations of all things in their surroundings, including, but not limited to, other individuals. These tend to include empaths, clairvoyants, clairsentients, and clairaudient individuals.

- Y, for Youth-ing, the ability to slow down/stop the concept of time from affecting your human experience and body.

- ID, for Inter-dimensional aspects/quality, the part of our consciousness that, when awakened, allows us to experience other dimensions, other dimensional beings, and worlds.

- RV, for Remote Viewing, the practice of viewing areas or people (inside of them or outside of them), past, present, or future, using the mind.

- T, for Tuning, a quality that allows us to harmonize energy, past, present, or future.

- SBR, for Soul Braiding, a quality of our consciousness that allows us to integrate aspects of either our larger Soul or an aspect of another Soul into our physical being, to be able to help us in some way. It can be permanent or temporary.

- SB, for Smart Body, a quality of consciousness that enables the body to give us information about our physical body. This is often done through muscle testing,

- ICC, for Inter Consciousness Communication, a quality of our consciousness that enables us to communicate and transfer our consciousness with family members (common with identical twins), friends, animals, plants, the planet herself, and inter-dimensional beings and/or boundless forms, and/or inanimate objects such as paintings, rocks, as well as any being who has passed on.

These are just a few of the ways I have experienced consciousness in human form so far. I'm quite sure there are many more qualities of consciousness to be enjoyed, maybe even an infinite number, but from my limited awareness, these are the only ones I'm currently attuned to. Unfortunately, we are not educated to trust the unseen or invisible, and so these qualities are ignored by the majority and written off as imaginings, coincidence, déjà vu, or just plain craziness.

The process of awakening, going from unconscious programming to conscious modes of operating, is akin to watching a 3-D movie of ourselves without the glasses. Someone finally comes along and says, *"Are you nuts? Put these on!"* and hands you a pair of 3-D glasses. Suddenly, the whole film comes to life. Things start jumping out at you; it's interactive and engaging. It's what you've been missing all along. *How did I not see this before?* Not your fault, by any means; it's what we were taught and conditioned to ignore.

Soul-Mapping

All our experiences, thoughts, words, and emotions, past, present, and future, reside in what is referred to in some circles as the Akashic Record. I call it the "Quantum Ribbon," and it's the vast memory bank, encoded in a quantum plane of existence, of all your many lifetimes. In the past, we had not evolved enough to be able to support each other in this quantum way, because we had simply not evolved our collective consciousness enough; the collective conscious had not yet been co-created. Things work very differently today, now that we are co-creating new levels of consciousness together, and the collective consciousness carries within it aspects and qualities that can be more easily accessed by the individual.

I began to understand that we experience polarity in our current lifetime, as well as in all the various incarnations that we've had. From the handful of past lives I've recalled so far, I've lived many opposing dramas. In one life I was a peasant, in another a noble. In one, a man; in another, a woman. A hermit, an icon. An artist, a warrior. Rich poor. Died young. Died old.

On a macro level, these opposing incarnations offer perspective and a unique awareness into the Soul. In each lifetime we've ever had, we've lived many musings, had many yearnings. I believe that these appetites and fascinations remain in our consciousness and carry forward into our future lifetimes as well.

As our consciousness evolves, and our DNA increases in efficiency, it gives permission for a higher consciousness to influence us; we'll remember more, which will lead to the release from institutionally approved narratives. In some cases, the conditioning and trauma that people have had to fight was not just from this lifetime but was brought forth from other incarnations.

Seeing beyond the visible is a skill. To feel into the field that lies beyond what we call "reality" takes a certain adroitness. However, just because we can't see something doesn't mean it doesn't exist. We are surrounded by air, gravity, and germs, none of which we can see with the naked eye, and yet these *invisibles* have a dramatic effect on our existence, every minute of every day. So much so that, without two of these invisibles, we would die. Aren't you curious about what other *invisibles* are out there waiting to be discovered? I know I am.

Beyond our snug-as-a-bug sleeping bag of limiting psychology and beliefs is the unmanifested world. This reality isn't so much about learning to accept our power, but rather to be on humble terms with the boundless conscious core of creation, and to remember your power to co-create with it.

So far, I have mapped my Soul's journey back to the fifteenth century (and two incarnations from ancient Egypt). This has led me to incredible insights and understandings as to why I am the way I am.

I do advise caution when it comes to working with people who can access our past lives. They may be able to do so, but we must be careful what lifetimes and/or trauma we open. I had a very unpleasant scenario once where an energy worker opened one of my past lives when I was a tomb robber in ancient Egypt. Unfortunately, in that specific lifetime, I got trapped in a tomb and died a slow and awful death. Following that session, I became claustrophobic overnight. I couldn't fly, or ride the metro, or take tunnels underground. I had to take medication to be able to do any of those things, and it has taken me the better part of five years to work through this trauma…and I'm still not finished.

From my place of understanding, I recommend being highly selective with whom we work on past-life retrieval and being responsible with our curiosity. There are things we may not want to know or access! Curiosity can be our genius, but it also killed the cat.

I've had a few people ask me why it is that I seem to have access to so many aspects of my consciousness. I don't think they're special to me, by any means. I truly believe we all have access to the same infinite potential; it's whether you choose to tune into it or not that makes the difference. It's a conscious choice. This quote taken from George Bernard Shaw's play *Saint Joan* sums it up quite perfectly:

> Charles (The King): Oh, your voices, your voices. Why don't the voices come to me? I am king, not you!

> Joan (the peasant girl): They do come to you, but you do not hear them. You have not sat in the field in the evening listening for them. When the angelus (church bell) rings, you cross yourself and have done with it. But if you prayed from your heart and listened to the thrilling of the bells in the air after they stopped ringing, you would hear the voices as well as I do.

Sap of Life

You are the narrator of your life, and the narrative you choose to tell defines you; it's that simple. *What story will you write for yourself?* We're conditioned and influenced by the context in which we live, and sold the misleading idea that it's not safe to follow our hearts and instincts, but to me, that's the safest and fastest way to fulfillment. Following your inner guidance and higher consciousness is not only safe, it's also very rewarding; it's freedom from suffering.

Solitude was necessary for me to rediscover who I was. Through my many years of inner shadow work, I stumbled about in my labyrinth of darkness and found many fragments of myself. I then brought them back to the light to become whole. I saw the illusion and brought it back for realization. I recognised the self-made prisoner and led it to liberation. I met the thief and the goody two-shoes, the wife and loner, the adored child and the neglected child, the beautiful child and the ugly duckling. I met fear and surfaced it to freedom, I met presence and absence, heard noise and yearned for silence. I identified misalignment and alignment, connection and disconnection. I am resilient and accept the ebb and flow of the polarity of this human experience. And above and beneath it all is the awareness of an all-encompassing, creative love and intelligence. Clarissa Pinkola Estés' words in *Women Who Run with the Wolves* rings so true, "When you have the courage to face the Unknown, you're rewarded with the light of Understanding."

Imagine a glorious tree. As a proud Canadian, I suggest one of our national icons—*the maple*, a symbol of unity, tolerance, and peace. *You* are the maple tree. The golden sap, that sweet elixir of life, flows inside you. Tap into it and allow the sweetness of your consciousness and Soul to fill your entire being. You can tune into this boundless Source all year round, every day, every moment. It's your point of power, and is ever available in the present moment. It overflows with abundance and wisdom and will set you free.

Brené Brown, professor, researcher, and storyteller, once remarked, "I now see how owning our story and loving ourselves through the process is the bravest thing we will ever do." I agree 1,000 percent! It's not always pretty or comfortable, but it's better than spending our entire lives defending an unconscious fictional character we didn't even write. When we are in alignment and acceptance, we can laugh a little more, dance a little lighter, play the music of our Soul a little louder. And if we're successful, then maybe we'll waltz through this whirlwind of a life with some ease and grace. As someone once said, "We're all fools whether we dance or not, so we might as well dance."

I came to understand that some people were made uncomfortable by the fact that I no longer had a box. It didn't make sense to them, and they'd much rather I had one so they could relate to me. I wasn't confined to any country, any organisation, or any person. When we awaken to ourselves, we cannot be enslaved, and we're not easily enchanted by the beguiling dream. Unless you're a chocolate truffle, what's the point of a box?

These days, I simply try and let the winds of my Soul's awareness and creativity guide my vessel. Some days are smoother than others, but I've learned that I'm whole all by myself, and while some are troubled by this, there are also those who are curious and even appreciative of my journey, because they, too, crave unification with their Soul-self.

This part of the infamous poem "Ode" by Arthur O'Shaughnessy comes to mind:

> We are the music-makers,
> And we are the dreamers of dreams,
> Wandering by the lone sea-breakers
> And sitting by desolate streams.
> World-losers and world-forsakers,
> Upon whom the pale moon gleams;
> Yet we are the movers and the shakers
> Of the world forever, it seems.

Art in all its various forms—music, films, poetry, books, plays, paintings—is, in many ways, man's greatest triumph. It outlives societies and wars, presidents and politics. It awakens sleepers and endures centuries, sometimes millennia, as a reflection of the dreamer's dream.

In 2005, concurrent with the arrival of my greatest gift and awakener, my son, I found myself in an unfamiliar partnership. I was so saturated with love for him that I began to shed the fortress of cultivated ignorance and conditioning that had enslaved me for so long. That love began to seep through my porous design, and I began to fall in love with myself. Like any new relationship, it required a lot of time and devotion. Instead of handing my power over to another, I decided to reclaim it for myself. I regained my inner strength and discovered my self-worth and self-love for the first time in nearly two decades. And more surprisingly, I went from atheist to mystic. As Shakespeare so wisely wrote in *Hamlet*, " …we know what we are but know not what we may be."

I learned over the years that the world is not what I was taught it was. Once you've had enough of all the unnecessary suffering, you begin to conquer your ingrained responses. You give it all up and finally surrender to your greater Self. Healing is the end of conflict with yourself, and well worth the reward of freedom and personal authenticity. Esther Hicks once said while channeling the entity Abraham, "Authentic power is when you're in alignment with your higher consciousness and when your personality comes to fully serve the energy of your Soul." I was, and still am, unlearning all that my conditioning context taught me to be.

Life is a mysterious theatre of dichotomies, polarities, and a wild cast of characters. Not everyone you trust will be loyal, and not everyone you love will set up camp with you. It truly is an endless Shakespearean drama, playing out one life at a time. Once you recognise this and understand that your attention has been misdirected to the outside world, you can kick back and have a good laugh. You'll hopefully chuckle at the outrageous scripts people are writing themselves, the wacky wardrobes, and curious hairdos. I believe that's why the Buddha laughed as he did. *Did he see the foolishness of it all, the sheer ridiculousness of the illusory world?*

Nothing should be taken too seriously, and *perfect* is a concept that has no place in this wacky world of theatrics. The human experience is a coin with two inseparable sides–one side is of love, magic, and limitless creative potential, and the other, of fear, logic, and restricted awareness. Contrast and creativity pulse through the veins of everything physical and etheric, drawing us towards two things: love and co-creation.

On these pages, I have shared with you some of my most personal struggles because, for all I know, they may not pertain to just me. I admit the act of writing this book is a selfish and cathartic one. As Maude Petre, an English Roman Catholic nun and writer, so eloquently put it, "True confession consists in telling our deed in such a way that our soul is changed by the telling of it." That has been true for me. I am a different person today than when I began writing this book eight months ago. And most importantly, I am now aligned with my truth more than ever before—this has given me a great sense of liberation.

Sharing our truth is probably the most intimate thing we'll ever do. People confuse intimacy with sex, but intimacy is about truth. When we stand in front of someone and share our deepest and most sacred truths with them, and they respond in a way that tells us our truths are safe with them, then we'll have found true intimacy. Sharing my journey with you is, in and of itself, a deeply intimate act.

The nature of the world is like a symphony. There doesn't seem to be a destination, per se, just a constant unfolding of harmonies, one note at a time. Evolution and expansion, creation and transformation. The young music prodigy Alma Deutscher is able to pick just a few random musical notes out of a hat and create the most incredible melodies. That's what we are all doing every day, moment to moment, sometimes consciously, sometimes unconsciously. We pick thoughts and desires from our life experience and create incredible rendezvous based on those choices.

Everything in the natural world seems to be doing it. You plant a seed and it transforms into a flower; you lay an egg and it becomes a bird. It would seem that we are all connected through a series of cooperative components, at a microbiological level, as well as on a macrocosmic level. We constantly unfold our Soul into being and more being, the expansion and never-ending notes of music that simply play on. A network of coefficient and infinite parts connected through the synergistic glue of life called "consciousness."

Jason Silva, public speaker and futurist, talks about towing the line between chaos and order, discipline and surrender, and how the artist summons them back into coherence and articulates them for us to see. Hilma af Klint, Swedish painter and mystic, did exactly this with her incredibly beautiful abstract paintings in the early part of the twentieth century. She brought back the unknown, the invisible, for us to witness. She bravely created work that was unlike anything the world had ever seen. It takes nerve to be you, unapologetically, and to lean towards your true potential, towards the unique symphony of your Soul song. It requires relentless action and participation and the subtle art of deep listening.

Contrast appears to be at the core of all vibrational matter and, when our polarities meet in perfect acceptance, we find ourselves in a sweet spot—in flow. Through my adventures with polarity and contrast, I've been able to find my way back to my true Self. I found self-love, alignment, and ecstatic flow. I found the wild woman Clarissa Pinkola Estés writes about, and I began to dance to the rhythm of her song. I continue to tear down my self-imposed walls of confinement and challenge myself every day to love and align with my authentic Self.

All things in this book are true, more or less, because everything is always subject to our individual awareness, consciousness, and perception. They are true to me. Either that, or everything I've experienced is nothing but lunacy from the depths of my mind. Ultimately, we are the authors and legends of our own dramas, fiction or fantasy, and it doesn't matter what anyone else thinks, just as long as *we* believe our story and our role as the hero. Just because no one else sees you as the ace in the deck doesn't mean you're not.

It's important to remind ourselves that spiritual insight is not a cure for all things. A vital part of our expansion is to develop our humanity just as much as our spirituality (if not more), and, for many of us, healing trauma is also required. My personal belief is that enlightenment is proved by our humanity, by how we respond to life and to people, not by our spiritual experiences. The more playful we are, the easier it is. So *let's go crazy*, as Prince urged, and dare to be the genius of our lives. We are all Shakespeare and Einstein with amnesia, after all.

In conclusion, my fellow truth-seekers, there is no right or wrong path to self-actualization; I'm not even sure that it's a destination. But there is only one way to pursue it, and that is to accept the invitation and dive in headfirst with no parachute. Open yourself up to awe and wonderment, explore the unexplored. When we have experiences beyond the familiarity of the mundane, we come face-to-face with the mysterious, with the unknowable. These enchanted moments catapult us into mystical experiences and awaken our minds. Our consciousness arises from a realm of boundless, infinite creative potential. I encourage you to embrace encounters that breach the norms of conformity. They light up our achromatic lives and remind us of what we've forgotten: that we are more than our egocentric consciousness, more than our m-Ego, and that we are interlaced with divinity. There is so much more to us and this world than meets the eye. Be committed to the exploration the way you're committed to your morning coffee.

Consider what lies beyond the simple systems of survival that we've created for ourselves. I cannot speak for you, but I have encountered wonderment, awe, rapture, alignment, flow, love, peace, awareness, and other dimensional entities. These tantalizing brushes with the *invisible* allow us to surrender from the limitations of our own minds and the limited belief systems we're so happily married to. Take the time to invest in the relationship with your bigger Self, and have the courage to express your true authentic nature with the world.

Coming home to Self is a never-ending game of hide-and-seek between polarities. An eternal tug-of-war between the m-Ego and a-Ego. Between the Ego self and the conscious Self. Between love and fear. *Is the juice worth the juicing?* Absolutely.

Printed in the United States
By Bookmasters